CONTENTS

With good Wishes

Mine.

6.9.2022

ST PATRICK'S, LIVERPOOL

By a paradoxical coincidence, researching and writing about the impact of the 1847 Typhus Fever epidemic in Liverpool took place during the lockdown imposed in response to the Covid-19 pandemic in 2020. Accordingly, it seems only fitting that this book should be dedicated to all those who died in both emergencies, their families and those who cared for them.

ST PATRICK'S
PARK PLACE
LIVERPOOL

A PARISH HISTORY
1821–2021

MICHAEL O'NEILL

GRACEWING

First published in 2022 by
Gracewing
2 Southern Avenue
Leominster
Herefordshire HR6 0QF
United Kingdom
www.gracewing.co.uk

ISBN 978 085244 981 3

Typeset by Gracewing

Cover design by Bernardita Peña Hurtado
based on photo by David Nathan
of the restored statue of St Patrick

LIST OF ILLUSTRATIONS

22. Peter Roberts Vault, 1828: Door.
23. Peter Roberts Vault, 1828. Interior with five coffins.
24. Overcrowded Room, 1847.
25. The Ten Roman Catholic Clergymen who died of Typhus Fever in 1847.
26. Canon Edward Kenrick, 1851–1860: Memorial Plaque.
27. Sixth Station of the Cross: Kenrick Memorial.
28. Fr P. J. Phelan, 1860–1864.
29. Fr J. Hawksworth, 1864–1868.
30. Canon Edward Goethals, 1868–1921: 1899 Portrait.
31. Monsignor James Nugent with the Fifth Irish Volunteers outside St Patrick's before embarkation for the Second Boer War, 1899.
32. Fr William Weston, curate, 1914–1922.
33. Fr Michael Timmons, 1921–1928.
34. Canon Arthur Madden, 1928–1942.
35. Monsignor Laurence Curry, 1942–1975.
36. Fr Thomas Lynch, 1975–1977.
37. Fr Joseph Marsh, 1977–1981.
38. Canon Leo Stoker, 1981–1998.
39. Rialto Cinema, destroyed in Toxteth Riots, 1981.
40. Fr Patsy Foley, 1998–2002.
41. Fr Kenny Hyde, 2002–2008.
42. Fr John Southworth, 2008–2018.
43. Fr Silviu Climent, 2018
44. Boys from St Patrick's School, c 1900.
45. St Patrick's Choir, 1923.

Illustration 24 reproduced by kind permission of Wellcome Images. Illustrations 61, 62 and 63 reproduced by kind permission of Theia Drone Services.

ACKNOWLEDGEMENTS

HIS BOOK OWES its existence to the enthusiastic determination and encouragement of Fr Silviu Climent to mark the bi-centenary of the foundation of St Patrick's Church by researching and publishing a new history. I want to record a special debt of gratitude to my two collaborators, Kirk Williams, Senior Surveyor with the Archdiocese of Liverpool, who has contributed the chapter on the architecture of the building and Joanne Lewis, Head Teacher, who has provided an insight into current primary education realities in St Patrick's parish.

Special thanks are also due to Brian Plumb whose knowledge of the Archdiocese is unrivalled and to Neil Sayer, Archivist at Liverpool Metropolitan Cathedral. I am also grateful to Mgr George Mooney, Canon Leo Stoker, Fr John Southworth and Fr Philip Inch of Liverpool Archdiocese; to Canon Eddie Gubbins and Fr Dominique Minskip of Middlesbrough Diocese, together with their Archivist, David Smallwood; and to the administrative staff of the Archdiocese of Adelaide. George Dawson, Co-Archivist of the John Taylor Bellfoundry Archives has greatly aided our understanding both of historical and current issues relating to the church bell and the unusual structure in which it hangs. David Nathan has provided all the photographs.

My gratitude also goes to Janice Barnes of Virtual Secretary Services Direct for her unfailing patience and efficiency in producing the entire text.[1] As always, my

---

[1] See www.virtualsecretaryservicesdirect.co.uk.

wife, Sue, has been unstinting in her support. Any errors are mine alone.
Michael O'Neill
Liverpool
July 2021

Introduction

T IS A great honour that one of my first tasks as the ninth Archbishop of Adelaide is to congratulate the faithful of Liverpool on the bicentenary of St Patrick's Church whose first rector was one of my predecessors Bishop Francis Murphy.

The Adelaide Archdiocese owes a deep gratitude to its first Bishop, Francis Murphy, who accepted his appointment to Adelaide after others had refused.

When Bishop Murphy arrived in Adelaide in 1844 to begin his ministry there were no churches, schools or presbyteries and only one priest to assist him.

He set about tirelessly raising funds to build schools and churches. In 1856 he began the building of St Francis Xavier's Cathedral, the oldest Catholic Cathedral in Australia, but he died before its completion.

Burials within the city square mile of Adelaide are prohibited but special permission was granted to allow Bishop Murphy to be buried in the Cathedral where he was laid to rest beneath the sanctuary.

A staunch defender of the Catholic faith, Bishop Murphy is remembered as a church builder. In December 1857 his last report to Rome summed up his work: '12 churches and six chapels have been built in the Diocese and two others are being built as well as a magnificent cathedral.'

He is also remembered as a builder of bridges between people. He came to Adelaide with an openness for everyone who lived here at a time when there was much tension between Christian communities and prejudice against the small group of Catholic pioneers.

He earned the respect of all, as evidenced by the large number of people who lined the streets for his funeral procession, including Anglican and other Protestant clergymen.

I welcome this opportunity to acknowledge his tremendous impact on the development of the Catholic faith in South Australia through the publication of this history of St Patrick's Church, Liverpool.

Thanks to Bishop Murphy, the ties between our two cities will always be there, as will the legacy that he has left us through his generosity of spirit and commitment to his faith.

In Domino
✠ Patrick O'Regan
Archbishop of Adelaide

Preface to 'Gleanings from the History of St Patrick's, Liverpool'

Attributed to Canon Edward Goethals

THESE MEMORIES, THOUGH to a great extent discon-
nected, of one of the oldest Catholic Churches
erected in Liverpool since the Reformation, will
be read with pleasure by the parishioners and friends
of St Patrick's. It would be a pity to keep them carefully
locked up to become gradually worn out by moths,
dust and time, instead of using them to some good
purpose. Even the apparently trivial events, sights and
experiences recorded in diaries of our holiday travels
are pleasing and delightful reminiscences. If the
records of St Patrick's were all of a similar nature there
might be reason enough for their publication. But this
history tells us of the persevering and successful
exertions of a band of Catholic Laymen, who,
prompted by the love of God and of his holy religion
in spite of many difficulties, erected a large and
commodious church principally for the benefit of their
poorer brethren; it gives a short but true and vivid
account of the Famine Fever, which in 1847 decimated
the Catholic Labouring classes, and it portrays the
heroic picture of the Liverpool Catholic Priests, who,
in imitation of their Divine Lord and Master, cheerfully
laid down their lives for the salvation of their flock.

Here we come in contact with that which is grand,
noble and inspiring, and an example of conduct, which
every Catholic Layman and every Catholic Priest

ought to follow, should similar circumstances present themselves.

St Patrick's, Liverpool, March, 1911

Rectors of St Patrick's

(Bishop) Francis Murphy, 1827–1837
John Walker, 1827–1830
George Gibson, 1830–1841
William Parker, 1841–1847
Canon James Crook, 1847–1851
Canon Edward Kenrick, 1851–1860
Patrick Joseph Phelan, 1860–1864
John Hawksworth, 1864–1868
Canon Edward Goethals, 1868–1921
Michael J. Timmons, 1921–1928
Canon Arthur Madden, 1928–1942
Canon Laurence Frederick Curry, 1942–1975
Thomas Lynch, 1975–1977
Joseph Marsh, 1977–1981
Canon Leo P. Stoker, 1981 -1998
Patrick Foley, SPS, 1998–2002
Kenneth Hyde, 2002–2008
John Southworth, 2008–2018
Silviu Climent, 2018–

Curates of St Patrick's

Roger Arrowsmith 1853–1855. Local conflicting factions led to his departure.
William Barnes 1905–1914.
John Berry 1884–1887.
Bernard Bimson 1971–1972.
J. Bowden Feb 1885-Aug 1887.*
William Bradshaw 1865–1867. A difficult career.
Joseph Buchanan 1890…died 1905.
David Bullen 1944–1945.
M. Burke May 1884-July 1887.*
Thomas Butler 1954–1962.
William Henry Byrne 1895–1904.
James Carter 1945–1953.
N. Cooke Oct 1909.*
Kenneth Davies 1960–1964.
George Dobson 1871–1875.
Vincent Doyle 1964–1970. Killed by train.
James Fanning 1884 … died 1909.
William Fayer Sep 1844–Oct 1846. Later in Salford Diocese.
Patrick Flynn 1870–1873. Became Rector of St Vincent de Paul.
Randolph Frith Oct 1842–Sep 1844. Later in Shrewsbury Diocese.
George Gibson 1829–1837. Rector 1837–1841.
Thomas Giles 1922–1927. Buried in Passionist grave.
William Godwin 1857–1862. Died of Typhus 1864.
Austin Gogarty 1971–1975.
Richard Grayston 1840–1847.
William Greene 1912–1926.

Henry Gregson Aug 1882–Apr 1885. Ordained as Cistercian 1870.

J. Haggar 1843–1847.

John Hanly 1880–1884.

James Hayes 1882–1884.

L. Hayes Aug 1896–Jan 1898.*

Jeremiah C. Holland 1863–1865.

Thomas Hogan Dec 1906-March 1907. Ill 1909–1933.

Michael Horan 1929–1930.

Philip Inch Sep 1987-June 1988

Philip Kavanagh Oct 1875–Aug 1880. May have moved to Birmingham.

Alban Kelly 1940–1946.

Denis Joseph Kelly 1928–1930.

Richard Kennedy 1865–1870.

Edward Kenrick 1847–1851. Rector 1851–1860.

Patrick Lynch 1899–1911.

Thomas Lynch 1972–1975.Parish Priest 1975–1977.

Gerald McCusker 1976–1977.

Peter McElhinney 1927–1929.

Francis McHardy 1931–1935. Incardinated 1931; from Clackmannanshire.

H. McIntee July 1873-Apr 1876.*

John Joseph McLaughlin 1927–1928.

Honorius Magini Feb 1859–June 1860. Scandal led to removal.

J. Maher July 1874–Sep 1875.*

Thomas Maher 1934–1944.

Martin Meagher 1960.

Denis Meehan 1943–1945. A boxing coach and chaplain to Aintree Racecourse.

Henry Falkner Milner 1900–1901.

Henry Vincent Moffatt 1929–1932.

Patrick Monagle 1932. Ordained 1930; on loan from Derry.

George Mooney 1957–1960.

M. Norris Aug 1876–July 1878.*

Henry O'Bryen 1858–1863. 'His polished oratory won unfeigned respect'.

Noel O'Connell 1958–1963.

D. O'Connor Aug 1887-July 1890.*

Denis Martin O'Dwyer 1951–1958. Parish Priest of St Malachy's 1966–1982.

James O'Dwyer Dec 1900–Oct 1906. Later in Lancaster Diocese.

Felix O'Hagan 1932. Ordained 1930; on loan from Derry.

Michael Joseph O'Neill 1867–1871.

Bernard O'Reilly 1847–1852.

Edward O'Reilly 1887–1892.

Edward O'Sullivan 1875–1878.

Patrick Joseph Phelan 1852–1860. Rector 1860–1864.

Cyril Francis Pilson 1933–1934.

Pierse Power 1847–1859.

M. Rea Aug 1878–July 1882.*

Joseph Rigby 1964–1971.

James Singleton 1860–1868.

James L. Smith 1887–1896.

Kenneth Smith 1946–1956.

Francis A. Soden 1868–1870.

Louis Verbrugghe 1893–1895. From Belgium.

Edward Walmsley 1850–1852. First Rector of St Vincent de Paul; died of Typhus.

Kevin Walsh 1946–1959.

Isaac Webster 1869–1872.

William L. Weston 1914–1922.

Thomas G. Wharton 1962–1968.

* These nine priests do not appear in 'Found Worthy'. Brian Plumb believes that they may be Irish priests who, like so many up to 1939, gave a few years to the 'English Mission'. All served during the incumbency of Canon Edward Goethals. Seven provided an almost continuous period of thirteen years' service. The Christian name of none of the nine is given in 'Gleanings'.

1 THE BACKGROUND

OWARDS THE END of the eighteenth century, the population of Liverpool had begun to grow rapidly, partly because of the town's importance as a centre of expanding international trade arising from the process of industrialisation known as the Industrial Revolution; and partly because of immigration from Ireland. Henry Lacey's *Pictorial Liverpool*[2] provides the following population statistics:

    1740 26,063

    1763 37,017

    1801 83,707

    1811 94,736

    1821 118,972

    1831 205,974

The National Census of 1841 records a population of 286,487. Muir's *History of Liverpool* gives 376,065 for 1851 and 716,000 for 1902.[3] Between 1740 and 1841, therefore, the population of Liverpool had increased tenfold, bringing with it a rapidly growing need for more houses, schools, shops and churches and the consequent risk of public health emergencies in relation to water supply and sanitation arising from

---

2   J. Stonehouse, *Pictorial Liverpool: Its Annals; Commerce; Shipping; Institutions; Public Buildings &c : A New and Complete Handbook for Resident, Visitor and Tourist* (Liverpool: H. Lacey, 1844), pp. 116–117.

3   R. Muir, *History of Liverpool* (London: Liverpool University Press, 1907), p. 302.

overcrowding; poverty and crime would also present increasing difficulties for the local authorities.

Organised religion responded to these challenges with a determination to provide new churches and schools wherever necessary. In South Liverpool, this process began with the new Parish Church of St James, St James Place 1774–75, built and perhaps designed by Cuthbert Bisbrown. Built of red brick with stone dressings and with a galleried interior set on slender, cast iron columns, it was the first of three churches, each of a different denomination and all situated within several hundred yards of each other, as recorded in the Ordnance Survey Map of Liverpool, 1849.

The second building, sadly the only one no longer in existence, was Wesley's Chapel, Stanhope Street, opened in 1827 and with a seating capacity of 1350. Again built of red brick, but with a pedimented front, including round headed windows and Greek Doric Columns, its site, overlooking the River Mersey, is depicted in a lively street scene in Payne's print of 1829, clearly showing how it derived its nickname 'The Chapel in the Park'. Only its perimeter wall survives, surrounding the chapel graveyard in which 412 victims of fever were buried in 1847. When the housing surrounding it was cleared, the chapel was closed and demolished in 1970.

The third building is the Catholic Church of St Patrick, Park Place 1821–27, designed by John Slater. With its pedimented gable, stone dressings, round headed windows, Greek Doric pillars and galleried interior supported by slender, cast iron pillars, it shares many of the architectural features of its two companion churches; despite its large size, with a seating capacity of 1,800, it seems also to have been designed to be as inconspicuous as possible, with many similarities to a Nonconformist chapel. Its architecture will be considered in more detail in a subsequent chapter. What follows is the story of this Mother Church of South Liverpool.

2 RELIGIOUS CONTEXT

HE HISTORY OF St Patrick's Church can be traced back to 1816, a time when no Catholic dioceses existed in England. After the Reformation, England became officially a Protestant country and the new Church of England maintained the traditional structure of dioceses and parishes.

The practice of Catholicism became illegal with severe punishments, including execution for High Treason, being inflicted on those who stubbornly adhered to their traditional Catholic Faith. As centuries passed, the penalties became less severe; in 1804, for instance, it was no longer illegal to practise Catholicism but those who did so were subject to many restrictions: they could not, for example, take degrees at the Universities of Oxford or Cambridge. Between 1581 and 1688, therefore, the administration of Catholicism in England was, to some extent, an underground operation and the country was regarded as 'mission' territory, subject to Penal Laws and controlled by a series of Arch Priests and later Vicars Apostolic, who exercised many of the functions of a bishop. In 1688, Pope Innocent XI divided England and Wales into four districts or Vicariates, each headed by a Vicar Apostolic. Pope Gregory XVI subdivided the four districts into eight; and, in 1850, Pope Pius IX restored an episcopal hierarchy to England and Wales.

The French Revolution (1789) and the subsequent Revolutionary Wars (1793–1815) between England and France which followed had an impact on the practice of Catholicism in England, not least because the British Government provided refugee status and pensions to the many Catholic French clergy who were expelled from their native country because of their religious views and reluctance to accept government control of their church. A direct consequence for Liverpool was the arrival in England, in 1793, of the exiled and controversial French priest, Fr Jean Baptiste Antoine Gerardot. Having first begun to earn a living by teaching French in Liverpool, Gerardot soon realised that the growing Catholic population of the town (10,000 people in 1804), was outstripping the capabilities of its three Catholic churches to serve them. St Mary's, Edmund Street (1707) and St Peter's, Seel Street (1788) were staffed by Benedictine monks; the Chapel at Sir Thomas' Buildings (1788–1815), the predecessor of St Nicholas, Hawke Street, was served by the Jesuits. There was no secular mission in Liverpool but Gerardot, a secular priest and a foreigner, could see the need for a new chapel and therefore approached William Gibson, Vicar Apostolic for the Northern District, resident in Durham, but the person with responsibility for Liverpool, to inform Gibson of his decision to open a new chapel on Scotland Road, dedicated to St Anthony which he did in 1804. Despite the misgivings of the native British clergy, Gerardot found that Liverpool people 'vied with each other to help a refugee French Catholic priest'.[4]

A precedent was set: the Catholics of North Liverpool had a new church; those in the town centre had a larger church when Fr Price at Sir Thomas' Buildings died in 1813 and his chapel was closed to be replaced

---

[4]   Details of his work may be found in an article by A. de Curzon 'The Reverend Father Gerardot and the "French Chapel" in Scotland Road, 1804–1832', published by the Historic Society of Lancashire and Cheshire in 1929, pp. 59–70.

by the Church of St Nicholas, Hawke Street, opened in 1815 on land donated by Liverpool Town Council; those of South Liverpool would soon be similarly provided for.

3 BUILDING THE CHURCH

NFORMATION ON THE building of St Patrick's Church may be found in a variety of sources. These include a short, illustrated history of the church, published in 1911, ninety years after its foundation, during the incumbency of Canon Edward Goethals; a further history, written to commemorate the 150th Anniversary of the church in 1978 by Anthony J. Hocter; Thomas Burke's Catholic History of Liverpool 1910; local contemporary newspapers such as the Liverpool Mercury; and original archival material at the Lancashire Record Office, Preston and in Liverpool. In particular, the Archives of the Archdiocese of Liverpool, situated below the Metropolitan Cathedral of Christ the King, contain a variety of documents and plans relating to the construction of St Patrick's.

Amongst these is the original, hand-written Minute Book of the Society of St Patrick 'established to bring about the building of a new Roman Catholic Chapel in Liverpool'. (It should be noted that, at this time, the term 'church' could only be applied to those churches operated by the Church of England—the established church. Places of worship maintained by other Christian denominations were technically known as 'chapels'.) The Minute Book records in detail the process by which the site for the new chapel was obtained, the finance organised and the construction undertaken.

The first general meeting of the members and subscribers of the Society was held at the residence of Mrs Glover in Whitechapel, on Sunday, 16th November, 1816. The names of 105 members were entered.

It was resolved that the following fifteen
members should constitute the Committee:
Messrs. John Byrne, Edward McNally, Richard
Rankin, Matthew Connor (Chairman of the
Society), Peter Houlgrave (Chairman of the
Committee), Luke Boyle, Joseph Birdsall, John
Bromley, John Reynolds, Thomas Billinge,
James Jeffries, Nathaniel Green, Daniel Mutch,
John Coghlan and Robert Houlgrave.

The first report of the Committee was submitted to the
members on Monday, 2 December, 1816. The report
states that the Chairman of the Committee had been
authorised to negotiate about the purchase of a suitable
site. Also, several plans for the proposed new chapel
had been submitted, and one had been selected 'combining elegance of appearance, economy of expense
and convenience of the structure, with dimensions of
a very large extent'.

The Society of St Patrick seems to have met with
considerable opposition at the very beginning of its
work. It was thought, by many, that the number of
Catholics in Liverpool did not warrant the erection of
a new church. On the other hand, Thomas Burke points
out that Canon O'Toole's Tables of Baptisms calculated
that there were 21,359 Catholics living within the town
boundaries of Liverpool, more than the capacity of the
existing chapels to serve them in 1811[5]. The members
of the Society came to very much the same conclusion,
basing their argument upon the published Table of
Mortality for the Town and Parish of Liverpool of the
Year 1815 and calculating that the Catholic population
would number about 20,000. As these figures were

---

[5] T. Burke, *Catholic History of Liverpool* (Liverpool: Tinling,
1910), p. 35.

very much called into question, the members of the Society immediately proceeded to take a census in order to prove, if possible, the correctness of their estimate. The result did not fully answer their expectations. The number shown by their census was 13,362.

In its response to this difficulty, the Committee provided an interesting insight into the place occupied by Catholics in the Liverpool community of 1815.

> First, that many of those engaged in taking the census were men in business, who had not been able to give sufficient time to ensure complete returns. Secondly, that to the number actually traced, should be added those who were prejudiced against the undertaking, those who, fearing that the inquiry was of a political nature, declined to give an account of their families, the Catholic servants of non-Catholic families, whole Catholic families in non-Catholic Lodgings, and others who must inevitably be missed in an inquiry of this nature, and the Committee come to the conclusion that they may safely put down the number at 18,000.

The response continued,

> A visit to most of the Catholic chapels-St Mary's, St Peter's, St Nicholas', St Anthony's shows the necessity of a new chapel. Frequently, you will behold numbers of Christians in the open air, and in the most inclement weather, complying with the obligation of attending divine worship, a sight which fills one with pity and admiration.

With renewed confidence, the Committee now moved on to the next stage of its task and reported:

The Society, anticipating no further opposition
or difference of opinion, have entered into a
treaty for the purchase of a piece of land in a
very eligible situation, and plans of a chapel
have been prepared, calculated to accommodate
1,200 persons upon the ground floor, free of all
expense, and containing in the gallery 106
benches, with accommodation for 600 persons.
The expense of carrying out the plan (including
the purchase money) is estimated at £9,000. The
Society is entirely dependent upon charitable
contributions, except in so far as they may be
assisted by the sale of seats in the gallery. If all
the seats were sold they would produce a sum
of £2,876, and yield an annual revenue of £370.
The poorest persons may have it in their power
to contribute by weekly subscriptions. The town
has been divided in districts, and persons have
been appointed for the collection in each district.

The Committee's fifth report is dated 23 February, 1817
and gives more details of the proposed site for the new
chapel, negotiations for the purchase of which had
been mentioned in their first report. The land was
situated on Great George's Street, facing Great
George's Place and extending back to Rathbone Street.
It is worth reflecting that, had the chapel been built in
this location, it would have been almost directly facing
the Parish Church of St James and so much nearer to
the centre of Liverpool that St Vincent's Church (1857)
would be most unlikely to have been built in nearby
Hardy Street. Ultimately, however, negotiations for
the purchase of this site failed as the owners, sensing
some urgency on the part of the Committee, had
increased the asking price.

Instead, negotiations began with representatives of the Earl of Sefton for one of two parcels of land, one in Upper Parliament Street and the other in Park Place. The latter, at 12/- per square yard, was more expensive than the 10/6 asked for the former; but, after heated debate extending over two meetings, the Committee opted for Park Place. The price of the site is recorded in the Committee's report of 21 October, 1818: £1,490, a sum which necessitated a rapid increase in collections at chapel doors and in the town districts. By this time, also, appeals for the necessary funds had been extended throughout England and Ireland; Fr Thomas Penswick of St Nicholas', who Thomas Burke says 'was the head and the front of the scheme for founding the church' gave it his enthusiastic support and John Slater was engaged as the architect.[6] His original line drawing of the High Altar and gallery layout is preserved in the Metropolitan Cathedral archives.

To a very large extent, the foundation of St Patrick's was a lay initiative: the Committee was made up of members of the local community who saw the need for a new church and took active steps to secure this aim, even to the extent of providing a future annual stipend of £370 for the maintenance of the clergy. They believed that their new chapel would bring benefits to the town of Liverpool as a whole; their stated aim, as recorded in their Minute Book (1816) is that it was:

> By no means the intention of the Society to confine this appeal to Catholics only ... they appeal to the charity of Christians of every religious persuasion on behalf of an object so closely connected with the cause of Religion, Benevolence and Social Order.

6   T. Burke, *Op Cit*, p.39.

Nevertheless, the Committee was aware of the importance of securing ecclesiastical approval for their
project, and, by 23 March 1817, Joseph Birdsall, one of
their members was recorded as 'having private business to attend to in the neighbourhood of Durham' and
was therefore 'deputed to wait upon the Bishop, with
a view to the removal of that uncertainty which existed
as to his intention of accepting or refusing the office of
Patron of the Society'. The bishop referred to was
William Gibson, Vicar Apostolic for the Northern
District, who had succeeded his brother Matthew in
this role and was in office 1790–1821. Now 79 years
old, and heavily dependent on his coadjutor, Thomas
Smith, with whom he had shared the trauma of the
French Revolution at the English College, Douai,
Gibson declared that he gladly accepted the office of
Patron, having been assured that it was intended to
give the nomination of officiating clergymen at St
Patrick's to the bishop of the district. In other words,
these were the terms on which he would sanction the
construction of the chapel.

It may be that Gibson and Smith were circumspect
in their response to Birdsall's proposal because they
wished to avoid a second controversy in Liverpool
following the difficulties they had experienced after
the exiled French priest, Jean Baptiste Antoine Gerardot had settled in Liverpool in 1804 and opened the
Church of St Anthony, of which he owned the freehold
and of which details may be found in the author's
history of the Church of St Anthony.[7] They would also
have been aware of the bitter dispute in Liverpool, in
the years after 1779, concerning the rights and respon-

---

[7]   M. O'Neill, *St Anthony's, Scotland Road, Liverpool* (Leominster:
        Gracewing, 2010).

sibilities of lay trustees and qualified bench-holders versus episcopal authorities in matters relating to clerical appointments and the control of mission finances. Gibson's brother, Matthew, set out the view of the church authorities very clearly: the claims of lay trustees would 'strike at the very being of ecclesiastical authority'; an issue explored at length in Peter Doyle's Mitres and Missions in Lancashire.[8] There was little possibility that Gibson would travel to Liverpool, given his age; he and Smith would leave the matter in the safe hands of Fr Thomas Penswick of St Nicholas', Liverpool, who would be consecrated bishop in 1824 and succeed Smith as Vicar Apostolic of the Northern District 1831–1836. Penswick would supervise the building of the new St Patrick's, for which Burke tells us he had already 'raised a considerable sum of money'; but also that he intended to 'frustrate the idea of the lay trustees to make the ground floor of the church free for ever'.

After four years, work had progressed to the point where the laying of the Foundation Stone could take place on 17 March, 1821. The ceremony was performed by Penswick, assisted by Gerardot, Rev T. M. Kirwan of St Michan's, Dublin and Rev James Dannett of New House, Aughton, all appointed by Gibson and Smith, with the sermon being given by Fr Kirwan. A detailed account of the proceedings is given in 'Gleanings from the History of St Patrick's, Liverpool', the short account published in 1911.

> In order to give greater effect to the ceremony, it was arranged that several Catholic Benefit Societies should join in a procession. At an early

---

8   P. Doyle, *Mitres and Missions in Lancashire* (Liverpool: Bluecoat Press, 2005).

hour, four of these Societies attended divine service at St Mary's, Edmund Street, the remainder with St Patrick's Society, at St Anthony's Chapel, Scotland Road. The procession formed in the following order:

Hibernian Society, 140 members;

Benevolent Hibernian Society, 64 members;

Hibernian Mechanical Society, 50 members;

Benevolent Mechanic Society, 50 members;

Amicable Society of St Patrick, 50 members;

Free and Independent Brothers Society, 40 members;

Industrial Universal Society, 120 members;

Catholic Charity School, Copperas Hill, 500 children;

Free School of the Benevolent Society of St Patrick, Pleasant Street, 472 children.

The procession commenced about 12.30 pm., from St Anthony's Place, through Scotland Road, Byrom Street, Whitechapel, Paradise Street, Duke Street, Cornwallis Street, Great George's Square, Upper Pitt Street, St James' Place, to the site of the New Chapel in Park Place, where it arrived a little after 2 o'clock. Six bands of music, the ringing of the parish bells, the many and costly banners, the numerous decorations of the vessels in the harbour, but above all, a bright unclouded sun, which shone forth nearly the whole day, with a moderate and refreshing breeze from the west, contributed to give a degree of splendour to its appearance, which can be but faintly conceived by those who did not witness it. The non-commissioned Officers and Privates of the 88th Regiment of Foot, or Royal Connaught Rangers, were marshalled in the procession by their own desire, and contributed one full day's pay in aid of the undertaking.

The procession was led by a series of carriages in which the clergy were seated. The account in the 'Gleanings' continues:

> It had been intended to place the procession regularly upon the ground; but upon its arrival, a scene took place which baffles description. The anxiety to obtain favourable situations, acting simultaneously upon thousands, the whole of the large area with the surrounding grounds, were in a few minutes completely covered; towards the spot where the foundation stone was to be laid, the crowd was so dense that it was with extreme difficulty a passage could be obtained for the Clergy. In the centre of the upper surface of the Stone a cavity had been prepared in the form of a cross for the reception of the articles to be deposited therein, consisting of a printed statement of the Catholic Chapels and Chaplains, with their respective Congregations in the County of Lancaster; and some recent specimens of printing, closely soldered up in a case of lead, over which were placed five deeply engraven metal plates, each measuring 13 by 8 inches. These filled up the shaft or upright part of the cross, in the arms of which were then placed a considerable number of silver and copper coins, enclosed in lead, comprising those of England and Ireland, of the Papal States and of several foreign countries, given by friends anxious to contribute a memorial of the event. A portion of Shamrock, the national emblem of Ireland, which had been blessed for the occasion, was next enclosed. The whole was then covered with a strong plate of lead and soldered down, in all probability, not to be again viewed by the eye of man for centuries to come. The procession was then again formed and marched away in the same order, in which it had come.

After its departure, a scene occurred, which no pen can describe, which none but the truly pious mind can appreciate, and which was more affecting, as it was totally unexpected; great numbers of persons who had remained until the departure of the bands of music had restored comparative silence, now begged that they and their children might be allowed to touch the Sacred Stone. The request was readily complied with by those to whose care it had been consigned; and so great was the concourse of persons, who desired this favour that it was necessary to appoint officials for the express purpose of marshalling their regular advance and departure from the interesting spot. Many approached with great reverence, imploring the divine blessing upon the undertaking. The manifestation of religious feeling continued until the approach of evening rendered it necessary to adopt measures for its safety. It was then enclosed with large stones, and covered with earth; and the more certainly to prevent its receiving damage, a strong guard was placed over it for the night, which was continued until the progress of the building placed it in security. The number of persons at the ceremony was estimated at 15,000.

Burke continues this account by adding that 'the festivities concluded by four public banquets held in Crosshall Street, Sir Thomas' Buildings, Ranelagh Street and Paradise Street'.[9]

As work continued, a series of distinguished priests, from Ireland and elsewhere, came to preach in the unfinished building—a process which could raise as much as £200 each time. The chapel's dedication to St Patrick recognised the growing Irish population of Liverpool, the significance of which could also be seen

---

[9]   T. Burke, *Op Cit*, p. 39.

in the inclusion of the Shamrock in the contents of the foundation stone and the implications for fund raising were clear; but controversy was to follow. Firstly, a rumour arose that Fr Penswick intended to place an English priest in charge of the Mission—one Fr John Walker of Ushaw was mentioned; but, when people's fears were allayed by the appointment of Fr Francis Murphy, the issue which had worried Gibson loomed even larger: what were the precise rights and responsibilities of the lay trustees in relation to the use of the building; how did this square with the wishes of the clergy and the needs of the poor? In the words of Burke, 'an angry correspondence sprang up in the newspapers and retarded the collection of the needed funds'.[10] Two of a series of letters which appeared in The Liverpool Mercury make this clear:

St Patrick's Chapel

As we plainly foresaw, we shall be inundated with communications on this subject; but as we have many other matters to attend to, we shall confine ourselves to facts rather than to declamation. It is our opinion and that of every other person with whom we have spoken on the subject, that the documents we published last week supersede the necessity of pursuing the investigation any further unless the Irish Roman Catholic can disprove the facts contained in those documents. The second letter of A Friend to Truth and Justice is written, however, with so laudable a view, that we here lay a portion of it before our readers, after observing to the writer, that it is not of so much consequence to ascertain who the traducer of Dr Penswick is, as to show that his assertions are unworthy of credit.

---

10   T. Burke, *Ibid*.

After asking the Irish Roman Catholic, 'whether he or any of his particular friends have at any time had any difference with, or suffered any disappointment from Dr Penswick, either before or after his advancement to the prelacy?' our correspondent proceeds as follows:—

I have felt deeply interested in the objects and the proceedings of the Society almost since its commencement; and unless it be the members of the committee or those immediately officiating in the common council, I have had as good an opportunity of knowing their plans as any other member of the community.

With this advantage in my favour, which I think the Irish Roman Catholic has not enjoyed, I presume I am better enabled to form an opinion as to the real bone of contention. I affirm that the love of power is the root of the evil; and I repeat here what I said in my last, that a few ambitious characters, grasping at power, and striving to eject those who are legally appointed, have brought the Society to its present distracted condition. I believe the ambitious few do not amount to half a dozen: they may have increased their progress, but I hesitate not to assert, and let anyone contradict me who can, that Bob Logic has been, is and will be, while a member, the constant disturber of the Society. Bob is well known as a famous club orator; and when such a man has a great deal of cunning and ambition, and very little reason, judgment or experience, much mischief may be done by his arts, in getting innocent and undesigning men to consent to his measures.

To begin with the first act of useless innovation, I ask the President if he knows any thing about it, who caused the committee, a few years ago, to be extended from fifteen to twenty one, even in spite of their legal adviser? Why, this very identical Bob Logic. From that very hour they may date their system of confusion. The aristocracy, if they may be so called, were turned out, the Trustees discharged, and the government of that excellent Society seized by three or four ambitious and imprudent democrats! Here, then, and at this time and place alone, 'dissentions' commenced the Trustees, who should not at any time be separated from the work, were dismissed and openly traduced and misrepresented by the very disturbers of the Society, Messrs Logic and Rhetoric, who behaved so ill to the first and respected Treasurer of the Society? Answer, Bobby and his beloved disciple!

As it is no part of my practice to misconstrue the acts of my neighbours; contrary to the opinions of many who have observed their course, I maintained and supported their claims to honest zeal and steady perseverance. But convinced as I now am of the folly and ambition of their acts, and assured that they have led the whole body into confusion, I am bound to state the truth in justice to a valuable Society, which it would be wrong to identify with their measures; in justice to the Trustees; and particularly in defence of the Right Rev Dr Penswick, who has neither act nor part in their dissentions. I hope I am incapable of 'setting down aught in malice' against any individual, however humble; but having written what I have written and seeing no reason to retract, it is my firm belief that the Bishop has no more to do with the existing disputes (but perhaps a great deal less) than the Irish Roman Catholic.

If the auxiliaries in the Chronicle will leave me to act on the defensive, I will undertake to bring my opponent to acknowledge his want of correct information, by substituting facts, instead of declamation, in support of my positions.

In conclusion, I sincerely hope that the chapel will be speedily opened; and in order to act justly, and meet the wishes of the people, I doubt not but Dr Penswick will appoint a talented Irish clergyman; and I hope he will be selected from the Rev Gentlemen who have already preached in behalf of the St Patrick's Chapel.

Yours &c

A Friend to Truth and Justice.

Christian Street, April 10, 1827.

St Patrick's Chapel

To the Editors

Gentlemen,

As you are always the friend of the poor people, I think you ought to show your friendship to us in the business of St Patrick's Chapel. We have paid our subscriptions to it these ten years, that we might have it to hand down to our seven generations; but now the Trustees will not let it be opened, as they won't be allowed to get it entirely into their own hands. I go to the Society now and then, and a couple of months ago the Society proposed to the Trustees to put half-a-dozen honest men in trust with them. But I am told they won't agree to that, and I do not see why; unless the Trustees think they would not be fit companions for them. Surely they ought not to object that the poor people who built the chapel should put as many honest men as they please to take care of it. The Trustees say now, they won't be satisfied in getting it entirely into their own hands; but they must also be allowed, when any of them dies, that the remainder of them must put a man in his stead. Now I think, Gentlemen, that this is very bad satisfaction for the people, for five men who have paid but little to the chapel to do as they like against the will of those who have paid much. Is it not plain enough, that if we allow them to put in whatever Trustee they please when one of them dies, they will soon be putting their wives and children into trust? And then it will be, when the frigate is built, a chip for the carpenter. We would soon be thrust out into the chapel yard, as we have been at the other chapels in town; but if we put in men of our own choosing, they won't let us be put out.

I am told now that the Trustees are to be arrested for debt due for the chapel, and that the Society would give them money to pay the debt if the Trustees would take any six honest men into their body, along with the money, or if they would go away and not tease the Society any more; but they have a faster hold than this, and they won't go away but go to law with the creditors; and if they do, why I could also say, the devil take them and their law altogether. I think, after all, the Trustees are honest men, but they have a bad way of showing it; for, if they would be good-natured to the Society, I am sure they would find many an honest heart among the 900 members that belong to it.

We have nearly all stopped paying to the chapel until it is opened, and I think there won't be much paid until then, so that it is a bad job to be losing the money at any rate; but we will all pay up again when every thing is settled to our liking.

So now I think, Gentlemen, the Trustees would do better to mind selling their TRUNKS, and their LIMESTONES, and their POTTED BEEF than playing my lord and master over St Patrick's Society, and keeping the chapel shut against us.

And they may take this with them, we will never let
them snatch it out of our fingers; we have paid
better to than they have done.

As you let the Trustees write for themselves, I hope
you will let me write for the poor people; for this
part of the business appears to be left to my humble
self, after all the fine scholars that have been
writing on the business.

Yours &.

An Old Subscriber to St Patrick's Chapel.

Liverpool, May 15 1827.

Unfortunately, no records or documents seem to have
survived, showing the work of the St Patrick's Society,
from 18 March 1821 to the end of May 1827. However,
a letter dated 19 July 1827 sent to Rev Richard Thompson, VG of Weld Bank by Joseph Birdsall, Honorary
Secretary of the Society states that they had now
received and expended a sum of money, exceeding
£7,000 and that the Committee still had to meet creditors' demands for almost another £3,000. To overcome
the financial paralysis arising from the dispute
between the Society and the Trustees, he had secured
the support of Penswick in having St Patrick's opened
for worship. There were two stages in this process.

First, as he understood that the Catholic population
of Liverpool and its surrounding areas amounted to
34,000 persons, a large scale financial appeal would be
organised, with Penswick writing the following circular letter:

A series of occurrences having retarded the long
expected opening of St Patrick's Chapel in this
Town, much dissatisfaction, which began to
manifest itself in a general suspension of weekly
contributions, has been the result. Measures are

now adopted to hasten the period when that spacious edifice will be dedicated to the purposes for which it has already received so large a share of public patronage. To that generous public, however, the present active managers are under the necessity of making another earnest appeal, on the success of which hundreds of their poor brethren depend for the means of attending religious worship. This is a fact to which I can bear testimony, and it may be rendered evident by a comparison of the number of Catholics in Liverpool with the places of worship hitherto provided for their accommodation. Such being the case, I recommend as highly deserving of support the zealous efforts of those who are soliciting aid to complete an edifice of which it may be emphatically said: Here the Gospel is preached to the poor.

THOS. PENSWICK,

Bishop of Europus and Coadjutor in the Northern District.

Liverpool, June 18th, 1827

The Bishop's appeal led to a series of fundraising sermons in aid of St Patrick's at the Liverpool Catholic Chapels on 15 July 1827, which raised £124 and donations began to arrive from chapels in the surrounding areas. Through these means, more of the necessary funds were secured.

Second, the problem of the nationality of the incumbent of the new chapel was neatly solved by appointing both the Irish Fr Francis Murphy, who moved to Liverpool from Bradford, and the English Fr John Walker from Ushaw.

4 THE OPENING OF THE CHURCH

HE HISTORY OF 1911 (*Gleanings*) provides a short outline of the formal opening of St Patrick's Church:

> The Solemn Opening of St Patrick's took place on Wednesday, 22nd August, 1827. The sermon was preached by the Rev J. Walker. The price of admission tickets to the ground-floor was 1/-, to the gallery 5/-. The admission receipts amounted to £142, and the collection to £107. Another Sermon was preached by the Rev F. Murphy, on the Sunday following, 26th August, and the receipts amounted to £109.[11]

Far more detailed accounts are provided by the *Liverpool Mercury* in an editorial and two accounts from individuals.

Opening of St Patrick's Chapel

This neat structure (the erection of which reflects so much credit upon the industry, zeal and astonishing perseverance of the middle and operative classes of the Irish Catholics of this town, to whose penny-a-week subscriptions, with the aid of the talents of some excellent and respectable individuals among the English Catholics it mainly owes its existence) was opened on Wednesday last with all the solemnity, splendour, and grandeur of effect so peculiar to the Catholic ritual.

---

[11] E. Goethals, *Gleanings from the History of St Patrick's* (Liverpool, 1910).

The ceremony commenced by the entrance of the Right Rev the Bishop of Europum, Dr Penswick, Coadjutor Vicar Apostolic of the Northern District, preceded by about forty of his clergy. The venerable prelate appeared in his full episcopal robes as high priest, with mitre and crozier, and preceded by deacon and sub-deacon. Mozart's solemn High Mass, No 12, so celebrated all over the musical world then commenced, and was performed with full orchestral accompaniments; to which was added, in the course of the solemn service, a selection from the sublime conceptions of Haydn and Bonfichi.

The vocal parts were admirably executed by Mrs Gillow, Mrs Corran, the Rev Mr White, Mesds Kelly, Messrs Gillow and Bennett of the Manchester concerts, with an excellent choir under the direction of Mr Henshall, who presided at the piano-forte, with Mr. Aldridge as leader of the band.

It is impossible for any lover of vocal music to pass over the admirable singing of the Rev Mr White. This gentleman, we are informed, received his education at the English secular college in Rome. His powers excited the admiration of the Romans and reached the ears of his Holiness Leo XII, who wished to retain him in the service of his choir, in the Sistine Chapel.

His voice frequently reminded us of Naldi, Angrisani and De Benis, chastened by religious propriety. We certainly never heard a finer bass; his style is pure, and his rich and mellow tones fill and long vibrate upon the ear.

An impressive and eloquent sermon, suitable to the occasion, was preached by the Rev John Walker, and a collection made to reduce the debt incurred by raising a temple, which evinces, in its construction, as much good taste as piety. If we were asked for a description of this chapel in two words, we should use 'simplex munditiis'.

We can bear personal testimony to the accuracy of the preceeding paragraph, which has been presented by a friend, and we take the opportunity of adding the expression of our entire approbation of the musical arrangements. The band was choice and complete, comprising Messrs Aldridge, Jackson, Tayleure, Rennie, Stubbs, Langhorn and others, to whose talents we have repeatedly borne testimony; together with the valuable addition of an excellent oboe. As we have never yet noticed Mr. Scruton, who plays this most delicate and difficult wind instrument in our theatrical orchestra, we take this opportunity of making amende honorable, by expressing the very high gratification we experienced on hearing his solos and masterly accompaniments. He is a most valuable accession to the theatrical orchestra—as there are very few even tolerable oboe players now in the country. Of the extraordinary powers of the Rev Mr White, who tendered his valuable services on this occasion, we feel called upon to offer a few observations. This gentleman is gifted with a voice which would prove to him a very handsome estate, if he were disposed to adopt the musical profession. We do not recollect being more pleased with the performance of any bass singer—not excepting Bartleman or Naldi. His voice bears some resemblance to the latter, but, in our opinion, it is softer. In all the transitions from pianissimo to fortissimo it never loses its character, but preserves a uniform sweetness and fulness which are very rarely united in the same individual. The band consisted of:

Instrumental

3 Primo Violins, 3 Secondo Violins, 2 Tenors, 2 Violincellos, 2 Double Basses, 2 Oboes, 2 Bassoons, Trombone, Double Drums, 2 Trumpets, Flute and Piano-forte.

Vocal

5 Trebles 8 Tenors 8 Altos 9 Basses.

We earnestly hope that the opulent Catholic gentlemen of this town and county will come promptly forward to defray the existing arrears which the erection of St Patrick's Chapel has entailed upon the spirited individuals who have at length put the poor Catholic residents in Liverpool in possession of an accommodation of which they stood so peculiarly in need; and as one means of raising the necessary supplies, we beg to suggest the occasional repetition of choral and instrumental performances, similar to those with which we were so much gratified on Wednesday. If a moderate price were fixed for admission, it is our opinion that a considerable sum might be raised by this means, and we could not resist the inclination we felt to urge the suggestion. – Editor, Mercury.

The following account of the ceremony is from another correspondent: as it enters more fully into certain particulars, we shall give it insertion.

To The Editors

Gentlemen,

If the subjoined hasty sketch be deemed worthy a corner in your publication, it is at your disposal.

This being the day announced for the opening of St Patrick's Chapel, preparations commenced at an early hour by the assembly of the different Hibernian societies in the town, with their banners and other insignia, with which, towards nine o'clock, they approached the edifice so long for them a principal object of care and solicitude.

About ten o'clock the congregation arriving at the church was numerous, and in a short time the ground floor was completely filled. For the present occasion only, the admission to this part of the chapel was judiciously regulated by tickets, charged at 1/- each, which tended materially to promote that order and regularity which it would otherwise have been almost impossible to preserve, had indiscriminate admission been permitted.

The assemblage in the gallery consisted principally of the representatives of the wealthy portion of the Catholics of the town and neighbourhood, together with a considerable number of highly respectable individuals of other sects, the whole embellished with an interesting portion of the fair sex, and forming, on the whole, a very genteel audience.

At a quarter past ten o'clock the Reverend Gentlemen who were to participate in the solemn ceremonies of the day commenced their ingress towards the altar from the adjoining vestry. The Right Reverend Doctor Penswick was the officiating Pontiff, and was attended by five Deacons, who, with him, entered within the sanctuary, to participate immediately in the celebration of the solemn office. The Right Reverend Gentleman was robed in his pontificals, as were also his Reverend coadjutors in the habiliments adopted to their respective stations.

They were followed by twenty nine other Catholic divines who arranged themselves around the rail which environs the sanctuary; and the whole had certainly a most solemn and interesting appearance.

Nor must we omit to notice the rare assemblage of talent, both natural and acquired, which so highly graced the orchestra; among this portion of the assembly were recognised many of the most esteemed vocal and instrumental performers of this vicinity – whose accompaniments, with the religious ceremonies of the day, constituted no trivial portion of the entertainment.

High Mass having commenced, it proceeded with that soul-subduing solemnity for which the rites of the Catholic Church are so eminently distinguished. The congregation kneeling, the Kyrie Eleison and Gloria were gone through;—the choir executing the pieces connected therewith in a most enchanting manner.

At this stage of the service, the Rev J. Walker entered the sanctuary; and having obtained the Bishop's benediction, approached to and ascended the pulpit at twenty minutes past eleven. His text was chosen from the 8th Chapter of the Third Book of Kings. He commenced with an appropriate description of the dedication of Solomon's Temple; his exertions at this point were striking and impressive, although the effect was, at times, to some degree lost to the audience in the more remote parts of the building.

Having then noticed the Society of St Patrick, to whose exertions the new chapel owes its erection, and having alluded to the satisfactory manner in which all the angry feelings had subsided, which lately agitated that Society, the Rev Gentleman proceeded to illustrate the nature of the Eucharistic Sacrifice. This part of his discourse being addressed, as it was, to a mixed audience, required, doubtless, no inferior degree of talent to dispose of, without offence to his 'Separated brethren' and this was effected in a manner eminently divested of that sectarian acerbity which too often distinguishes the assertion in public of any peculiar doctrine.

Allusion then being made to the highly-valued exertions of the labouring classes of the Catholic community of Liverpool, as well as the generous benefactions of the more opulent classes in erecting this temple, the Rev Gentleman paid a handsome tribute to the characteristic zeal of the sons of the sister Isle, and warmly eulogized their indefatigable industry and perseverance in promoting the faith of their fathers. He then summed up in a very animated, impressive manner. The delivery of the sermon occupied forty-two minutes.

It may be worthy of remark here, that the Rev Mr Walker's talents as a preacher are by no means of an humble order. His style is dignified, and his delivery remarkably free and unrestricted, whilst his manner is ingenuous, and his sentiments correct and well adjusted. With enunciation somewhat more full and distinct than was exhibited today, he would doubtless prove a very attractive magnet at the south end of the town.

The sermon being concluded, the ceremonial part of the service was again resumed. Previously to the Preface, a short hymn, which, to an English ear, had the sound of Italian, was executed in admirable style, as was also the Credo, the Agnus Dei &c. But it would require the pen of a Mozart to convey any thing like an adequate idea of the effective manner in which the musical part of the performance was executed.

The Bishop, leaning on his pastoral crook, concluded the ceremonies by giving the benediction; shortly after which the congregation dispersed, it being then a quarter past one.

On the whole it may doubtless be truly remarked, that such a refined intellectual treat has seldom, in Liverpool, been witnessed, and is still more rarely surpassed. The tout ensemble reflects certainly very considerable credit on the good judgment displayed in arranging the ceremonial; and, no doubt, but the funds for liquidating the debts on the building will have no small benefit accruing. The receipts have not yet been officially announced, but they will probably not fall short of £300.

If one feeling of regret can on this occasion arise, it must be only that similar means of promoting the other charities of the town are not more frequently resorted to; the means are most effective, while they are at the same time wholly unexceptionable, and therefore worthy (of) the attention of the constituted authorities.

This sketch, too hasty perhaps, and unpolished, is submitted by a person having no other connexion in the affair than that of a casual OBSERVER.

Liverpool, 22nd August, 1827

The Chapel was now officially open; the next three years would see concerted efforts to complete and pay for the building and its contents.

5 THE PROJECT COMPLETED

GAIN, THE HISTORY of 1911 ('Gleanings') provides invaluable information.[12]

In a printed address, dated 27th September, 1827, of which 5,000 copies were distributed, the Committee made another appeal for help, and concluded with the following remark: 'It has been observed that large numbers frequent the ground floor of St Patrick's Chapel who, it is well known, can, without inconvenience, contribute to the expense which has been incurred. This free accommodation was originally intended for the poor only'. Less than two years later, that word 'originally' would be the subject of fierce controversy as the terms of the Lease of the Chapel were negotiated; the outcome may be seen on the west front of the building where, engraved in the stone plaque is the legal requirement that the ground floor 'should for ever remain free'.

On 18th January, 1828, the Committee reported that a sum of £2,500 was required to meet their creditors to the full, and they suggested that some 250 Catholics should be asked to lend at least £10 each, free of interest, to be repaid weekly, casting lots for the first repayments of the sums lent. 'Till this debt is discharged, the Committee cannot see their way to commence the erection of a school and Presbytery.'

This method of fund raising may not have proved fast enough to satisfy the remaining creditors, if we

---

12   E. Goethals, *Gleanings from the History of St Patrick's* (Liverpool, 1910).

are to judge from the following entry in the Minute Book:

> 28th October, 1828, it was resolved that the Committee of the Society of St Patrick be instructed to enter into a communication with the Trustees to inform them that the Vicar Apostolic of the Northern District and the Incumbents of the Chapel, are, it is believed, ready to advance the whole of the money due at present, on the estate, on conditions that are highly satisfactory, and to solicit the advice and help of the Trustees in the important negotiation. The following are some of the conditions of the proposed negotiation:
>
> 1st ... 'That the Bishop shall advance the necessary sum for the payment of the outstanding debt, including the land, provided the Deeds be given up to him and the Incumbents conjointly.
>
> 2nd ... That the Incumbents shall agree to unite with the Society in making every effort to commence immediately the purchase of a piece of land, and the building of a school thereon.
>
> 3rd ... That the Incumbents shall further engage to procure an organ, beautify the Chapel, light it with gas, and plant trees around it.
>
> By the removal of the remaining debt £1,800, the Chapel and Estate will rest on a secure foundation.'

The 'secure foundation' is probably to be found in the Lease which was eventually agreed between the Committee and the Vicar Apostolic, some of the terms of which are different from what is suggested in the Minute Book. The Lease sets out the legal status of St

Patrick's. It is dated 18th May, 1829 and is an agreement between Alexander Ryan of Harrington (Toxteth), Lime Burner, Matthew Connor of Liverpool, Trunk-maker, other Members of the Society and the Rev John Walker and the Rev Francis Murphy, both of Harrington on the one part and the Right Reverend Thomas Penswick, Doctor of Divinity and other senior clergy on the other part. It states that, in consideration of the sum of £2,000 being paid by Penswick and his associates to Ryan and his associates, the land on which St Patrick's stands will be leased for a term of 5,000 years, at a peppercorn rent ('if demanded'), on condition that Penswick, his associates and their heirs covenant that they will

> at all times, and from time to time, during the continuance of the term hereby demised, well and substantially repair and keep repaired ... at their own expense and costs all and singular the inner parts of the said demised premises ... and also all and singular the outside brickwork, plastering, slating, tiling, railing and other parts of the said Chapel, Building and Premises ... and shall and will preserve the inscription engraved upon stone (as set out below) ... fixed in the outward wall in the west front of the said Chapel in as good a state of preservation as the same now is and shall not allow the same to be removed, altered or damaged in any wise however ... and will keep the Chapel insured ... and will not convert the said Chapel into any other building or suffer the same to be used for any other purpose than as a place of Divine Worship according ... to the rites ... of the Roman Catholic Church.

SAINT PATRICK'S CHAPEL
Built by Public Subscription under the express
stipulation that the whole of the Ground Floor should
for ever Remain free for the Accommodation of ALL.
'Keep therefore the words of this Covenant and fulfil them.'
Deut XXIX 9
Begun AD 1821
Finished AD

The negotiations over the uncompromising terms of
this lease seem to have been protracted. Nevertheless,
on 28th December, 1828, the Committee, in what they
term the last report, mention 'that they had till now
received by collections, sermons and legacies, a sum
of upwards of £9,000. The Committee, before ending
their labours, consider it but right to express their deep
obligations to Mr M O'Connor, from whom originated
the idea of St Patrick's Chapel, and recommend, at
least for some time, a suspension of their work'.

On 9th May, 1830, the Reports of the Society contain
the following resolution: 'That the Society having now
honourably concluded the undertaking of raising
funds for the Organ, its exertions shall now be directed
towards the raising of funds for the purchase of land
and the erection of a school'. There is no mention of
the purchase of the Presbytery at 22, Park Place, a
building which still exists, directly opposite to the
church with its ceremonial pillared balcony above the
fanlight of the front door.

Despite the statement made about 'ending their
labours', reports of the Society making weekly collections continue down to 21st October, 1830.

6 Early Years and Challenges
1827–1868

HEN St Patrick's came into use in 1827, it was under the authority of the Vicar Apostolic of the Northern District, one of the four districts into which England was divided. There were no parishes in the twenty-first century sense; each chapel constituted a Mission, led by one or more Incumbents who had little security of tenure. One of a group of priests might be known as the Senior Priest. The system was modified in 1852 when certain missions received 'Missionary Rectors' who were almost irremovable. In 1908, missions finally became known as 'parishes', each led by its own parish priest.

Fr Francis Murphy was the first of the Incumbents of St Patrick's, a role he shared with Fr John Walker. Francis Murphy (1795–1858) was born in Navan, County Meath; his father was a brewer. He was ordained at Maynooth in 1825 and volunteered to work in Bradford from where he was transferred to St Patrick's in 1827. He volunteered to work in Australia in 1837 and, in 1844 he was consecrated as Bishop of the new Diocese of Adelaide where he went on to build twelve churches, six chapels and the Cathedral of St Francis Xavier, where he is buried. Tall and sandy haired, he was a skilled preacher and a strong opponent of alcohol.

The *Liverpool Mercury* shows how diverse was the large community served by the new church, as may be seen from the following press reports.

Liverpool, Friday, 24ᵗʰ December, 1830: Charity Sermon.

On Sunday last, at St Patrick's Chapel, an eloquent appeal in aid of the funds of the St Patrick's Benevolent Society was made by the Rev F. Murphy, one of the incumbents of the chapel. The Reverend Gentleman drew a frightful picture of the misery and destitution of many of the poor creatures whom he visits in the discharge of his pastoral duties. He stated that many of them could get nothing but potatoes and water, and that only once a day, whilst others could not even get that miserable sustenance; that, in some instances, when the father of a family had been stricken with sickness, every disposable article of bedding and clothing had been disposed of, and the miserable creatures were lying on the cold and damp floors of their wretched cellars. The collection amounted to £34. We scarcely know of a charity more deserving of support, or on which there are greater claims than the benevolent Society of St Patrick.

Liverpool, Friday, 21ˢᵗ March, 1834: Sacred Music at St Patrick's Chapel.

On Sunday last, a grand, or High Mass, was performed at St Patrick's Chapel, and a sermon was preached by the Rev Mr Murphy, who forcibly and eloquently appealed to his hearers on behalf of the Catholic Charity Schools, for which a collection was afterwards made. The music was most admirable: and the choir had the advantage of the talents of Madlle Cesari, Signor Deval, and Signor Marani, whose voices were heard to admirable effect, as the chapel appears to be peculiarly well adapted for the purpose. Mr Webbe officiated at the organ with his usual taste and discrimination: and, upon the whole, we have seldom experienced a richer treat.

We subjoin a list of the pieces performed on this occasion, and the names of some of the singers:

'Laudate' by Zingarelli–Tenor, Solo, and Chorus, Monsieur Devin.

'Kyrie' Mozart, No 12–Tenor, Bass & Chorus, Signor Deval and Signor Marani.

'Oh, Signor' Rossini, Soprano Solo, Mademoiselle Cesari.

'Credo' Mozart, No 12–Tenor Solo and Chorus, Signor Deval.

'Offertorium' Mozart, Signor Deval.

'Sanctus and Benedictus' Mozart, No 12–Tenor, Bass and Chorus, Sig Deval & Sig Marani.

'Agnus Dei' Mozart, No 12–Soprano Solo and Chorus, Mademoiselle Cesari.

'Trio' Pacini–Mademoiselle Cesari, Sig Deval and Sig Deval.

The choruses were very effective; but as the names of those who composed them were not furnished us, we cannot enumerate them.

All of the singers mentioned were prominent musicians in Liverpool of the 1830's. Monsieur Devin, for instance advertised in Gore's Directory of Liverpool (1834) that, at his Academy, No 3, Grenville Street, Great George Street, only half a mile from St Patrick's, he offered French Language, Singing and Spanish Guitar lessons. It would seem that Webbe, with his national reputation as both organist and composer, and attracted to St Patrick's by its fine new organ, surrounded himself with an excellent group of performers to accompany the solemn liturgies of the church.

Fr John Walker (1801–1873) was born in Lancashire and ordained at Ushaw in 1826. He preached at the opening of St Patrick's, where he served from 1827 to 1830. He became ill and had to return to Ushaw; after his recovery he was appointed to St Peter's, Scarborough where he replaced the 1809 chapel in 1858 with a new church by Goldie, in which a large memorial records that he was pastor of its Catholic flock for thirty eight years, dying as a Canon of the Diocese of Beverley in 1873.

When Fr Walker left St Patrick's in 1830, he was replaced by Fr George Gibson (1806–1875). Gibson was born in Manchester and, after ordination at Ushaw in 1829, served at St Patrick's until 1841. He spent five years as a missionary in Africa until 1846, and, after a year at St Gregory, Weld Bank, was Rector of St Mary's, Chorley 1847–1851; and Rector of St Mary, Hornby until his death in 1875. In 1836, the formidable John MacHale, Archbishop of Tuam, frequently referred to as the 'Lion of the Fold of Judah', visited St Patrick's and preached a charity sermon which raised £200. Little would he have realised that 140 years later, in the person of Fr Thomas Lynch, St Patrick's would have a parish priest from his own archdiocese.

That the church played its part in important moments in national life may be seen from the following brief report in the *Liverpool Mercury* for Friday 7th July, 1837, following the death of King William IV, the uncle of the future Queen Victoria:

The Last Lie Against the Roman Catholics

Friday 7th July, 1837

The following letter appears in the *Morning Chronicle* of Monday:–

Sir,–in today's *John Bull* I observe the following paragraph:–

It is confidently stated that the Roman Catholic priesthood, not only in Ireland, but in this country, have prohibited their flocks from wearing mourning for his late Majesty.

When I mention to you that in every Roman Catholic chapel in London the pulpit has been covered with black cloth, and that from every pulpit the Catholic priests have considered it a part of their duty to make such reflections upon our late national bereavement as the solemnity and sorrow of such an occasion demands, you will perhaps be kind enough to give insertion to this contradiction of a lie as gratuitous as it is malevolent.–I am, Sir, your obedient servant.

A Roman Catholic, Athenaeum Club July 2.

At St Patrick's Chapel, in this town, not only was the pulpit covered with black, but the wall behind the altar, also, to a considerable extent. The royal escutchion was also displayed above the altar. We believe that similar marks of respect to the deceased Monarch were also paid at the other Catholic chapels. What a contemptible cause must that of Toryism be, when such gross and glaring falsehoods are deemed of service to it!

The church also participated in the local religious controversies of the time, as may be seen from this report in the *Liverpool Mercury* for Friday, 9th March, 1838. Fr Parker was the newly appointed curate at St Patrick's.

Controversial Lectures–

We understand that it is the intention of the Rev Mr Parker, one of the officiating ministers of St Patrick's Chapel, Toxteth-park, to deliver a course of lectures explanatory of the doctrines of the Roman Catholic Church, on the Wednesday and Friday evenings during Lent. We do not suppose that there are at the present day many Protestants who really believe that the Pope is either Anti-Christ,–wears a tail, or sports a cloven foot, but we fear there are thousands who know nothing whatever of Catholicism but what they have heard from its enemies, and are therefore inspired, if not actuated by the strongest prejudices against both the religion and its professors. As a matter of common fairness all men, even if they be Roman Catholics, ought to be heard before they are condemned. We, therefore, feel particular pleasure in calling the public attention to the proposed course of lectures, especially as we understand that Mr Parker is an eloquent preacher, an excellent minister, and a man every way qualified to do justice to his subject. And as a specimen of the spirit in which he enters upon the task, we subjoin an extract from his address on Wednesday evening last, which we recommend to the especial notice of the Rev Hugh M'Neile and all zealots of his class:–'If it is charged against us,' said the Rev Gentleman, 'that we condemn to eternal perdition, without exception, every one who differs from us in religious belief, I should indeed blush for myself and for you, my dear friends, if I could fancy that such an uncharitable and unchristianlike impression could find a place in your minds. No, we believe and trust that many may and will be saved out of every creed, whether Catholic, Protestant, Quaker, Methodist, &c., who is so from education, and through conviction of its truth, and who thinks himself in the right way, and who would immediately embrace the most perfect if he had the opportunity offered of embracing the same. It is then to remove erroneous impressions received from long rooted prejudices by those who differ from us that I propose to enter upon a course of lectures during the Lent, explanatory of the doctrine of our holy religion, that I may at least effect so much benefit to a portion of society, that the canker which has so long infested their minds being cleared away, they may live with better feelings towards their Catholic brethren, and I respectfully invite all persons of what religion soever they may be to attend and listen to what I shall advance, and I hope that I shall not be found to utter one syllable of irreverence or disrespect of any creed whatsoever, however opposed it may be to that of my own, my soul object being charity and good-will amongst my fellow Christians.'

An indication of the volatile local conditions in the area around St Patrick's can be found in the issue of *Liverpool Mercury* of Friday, 7ᵗʰ June, 1839:

Alarming and Destructive Riots

The riotous and disorderly occurrences arising out of the proceedings of a few drunken and lawless carpenters, which we mentioned in our last, were, we are sorry to say, renewed with even greater violence on Friday. Early in the morning great excitement still prevailed, and crowds of persons assembled in New Bird-street and the neighbourhood where the greatest damage had been done during the riots of the preceding evening. In New Hall-street, close to New Bird-street, the newly opened Inn of Mr T. Lythgoe was broken into. The windows were smashed, and the rioters obtaining entrance beat not only the owner, who is dangerously injured in the head and body, but his daughter, a young married woman, who was so much hurt and alarmed, that she was removed to a neighbour's house in a state bordering on delirium. In New Bird-street, the public-house kept by widow Doran, and another near it, were severally visited. In Jordan-street, Davis's and Simpson's were equally attacked; and in Simpson-street, Crosbie-street, &c. similar destruction of windows and doors took place, some by one party, and some by the other. During the whole of the forenoon rumours of partial disturbances in the neighbourhood of the previous riots were prevalent, and the excitement consequently increased. Stones had been collected at an early hour, for attack or defence but no serious contact of antagonist parties took place for some time afterwards. Preparations, it was also openly announced, by the Irish inhabitants, were made to give a warm reception to any future assailants, a stronger feeling of animosity being excited by the fact that the grand attack made upon these houses on the previous evening was before they had returned from their work, and when they could neither defend themselves, nor allay the alarm of their wives and children. The police were early on the alert, and their patient exertions throughout were most praiseworthy, and we are glad to say, most successful. Some skirmishes took place in the early part of the day, but they were not of a formidable nature. In these, as well as in the previous and subsequent disturbances, we are bound to say that the females attached to the parties, and particularly the Irish portion of them, were unbecomingly active, many of them urging on the respective parties to whom they were attached, and not a few supplying them with arms and ammunition in the shape of sticks, pokers, stones, bricks, &c.

Amongst the rumours that got abroad was one,— that the carpenters were armed for the purpose of demolishing the Catholic Chapel of St Patrick in the Park-road; and the lumpers and Irish labourers needed no stronger incentive to embark in any undertaking, however perilous. They soon mustered in an immense body, and reinforcements were continually coming to their assistance from the north end of the town. Between three and four o'clock much uneasiness became apparent in the neighbourhood of the docks south of the Custom-house. At about a quarter before four a number of carpenters (chiefly apprentices) collected on the east side of the Salthouse Dock, when Mr Dowling, who came to the spot with a small body of police, addressed them, and requested them to disperse and commit no violence. They replied that if he would insure them protection in a house in Sparling-street, (Mr Fagan's) they would go away. Mr Dowling said he would. Mr Whitty afterwards came up with his force, and both went with them to Mr Fagan's, where they were left with a guard, on a promise that they would not come out. It appears, however, that others of the carpenters' apprentices afterwards drove to the house in a cab, with colours flying, and calling out "Where are the Irish now?" &c., so that a mob was collected, which resulted in the destruction of the windows. A small police force was soon on the spot, and paced the street for some time; but on their leaving (about four o'clock) several other panes of glass were broken. Shortly afterwards another disturbance occurred between the carpenters employed on the new Government steamer, lying in the Canning Dock, and some of the Irish dock labourers. The carpenters rung the yard bells, and, on being reinforced, proved victorious. It is reported that a man's arm was nearly cut off in this affray, by one of the carpenters, with an adze. The carpenters, after this, crossed the Salthouse Dock-gates, and at the south end of that dock another disturbance occurred. One man was pursued by another with an axe, and had he not leaped over the bow of the vessel to which he had run for safety, he must have been severely injured, if not killed, by the blow that was aimed at him. As it was, he was in danger of being drowned, but was saved by a boat. Meantime partial riots took place in most of the streets leading southward from St James's-street. The disposable police were summoned from the different stations.

Mr Highton (Mr Whitty's clerk) was in command of 16 men, and about a quarter-past four o'clock, while going down Park-lane, they were met by about five hundred Irishmen, some with spades and other instruments, but the most part with sticks of various sorts, and many of them of formidable dimensions. Mr Highton, and his comparatively inadequate force, passed them–filing on the footwalk. A few others of the body, however, joined them, and they all turned round, and followed the Irish, who had mostly been drawn from their abodes in the north end of the town by the rumoured pending destruction of St Patrick's chapel. On their way they were met by Mr Dowling, with a few other constables, who joined them. They then went at double quick pace to overtake the belligerents. The latter took down Sparling-street. Inspectors Angus, McGill, and Thompson, happened at the same time to be coming up the same street, armed with cutlasses which, however, they never used further than to show them. The mob being thus shocked, turned round, and were met face to face by Mr Dowling and Mr Highton's party. Being closely pressed, they presented front, and made an attack upon the police. They were soon, however, discomfited, and were in the end soundly drubbed. They dispersed and fled in all directions, several of them who were intercepted in their flight praying on their knees for mercy. Mr Dowling again assembled the men in the same street, and they proceeded to Park-lane. About a quarter past five o'clock, Mr Highton with Inspectors Angus, Thompson, McGill, and Donovan, and a force of 50 men, was standing at the top of Crosbie-street, when they heard shrieks of persons alarmed, and shouts of another mob. They saw, on looking down the street, a dense crowd approaching, and brandishing axes, adzes, mauls, bars of iron, sticks, and other weapons. They also saw bricks and stones sent forcibly at the windows and thrown back again. These were the carpenters, who had assembled by toll of bell, and they had taken the bricks from a new building which they had partly demolished. They had broken in about a dozen doors. Mr Highton here divided the men into four sections, each under an inspector, and they went at double quick time down the street. They soon came up with the carpenters. Mr Highton addressed them, requesting them to give up the weapons with which they were armed. While he spoke, they were gradually surrounded by the police. Several of them escaped with their weapons, but the greater number reluctantly submitted to be disarmed, force being in some instances required. Not fewer than 120 dangerous weapons were here accrued, including axes, adzes, pikes, bars and rods of iron, &c., besides a large number of bludgeons. The last were for the most part of hard and heavy locust wood, (used for treenails) split into rude squares, presenting sharp edges, and rounded at one end with the axe, to fit the hand. The whole of these weapons were placed in a cart, together with six prisoners, all taken in the act of throwing missiles, or being otherwise active in the riot. After clearing the street of the crowd, the police accompanied the cart to the Bridewell in Brick-street. They were met on the way by Mr Whitty, with another body of police, who formed in the rear and followed to the station, where the articles were deposited. The last noticed disturbance, in which the weapons was so spiritedly taken, was the most threatening and dangerous of the day. Meantime Mr Whitty was active throughout the whole district, and was the foremost in every post of danger that presented itself. He was constantly seen, on horseback or on foot, and carried nothing with him but a strong whip. His strong voice, and good humoured but determined manner, had a powerful effect in dispersing the crowds in various directions, who might otherwise have suffered injury from contact with the rioters, or forcible dispersion. The whole of the police employed were divided into six bodies, and it is remarkable that eight "general engagements" took place, all of which were "well fought"—great resistance being shown by the rioters in all, and great energy by the constabulary. We have heard it complained that in some instances the police laid about them violently and indiscriminately; but in the dispersion of mobs, or the often necessary clearing of streets of idle spectators on such occasions by comparatively a handful of men, it is impossible to avoid some slight injury to individuals who may be in the way, in the attempt to quell disturbances which threaten the general safety of life and property. Where undue violence may have been resorted to, the officers using it will, doubtless, be brought to account.

Amongst the numerous emutes quelled by the body headed by Mr Whitty, was a desperate affray at about half-past four at the corner of Simpson-street and Blundell-street, between large bodies of the belligerents. He went in amongst them at double quick pace; they fell back on each side, and did not escape without (what is far more exemplary in such cases than fine or imprisonment) a sound beating. Superintendents McDonald and Tyrell, who were with Mr Whitty, were also most active. The latter himself secured a man with a loaded pistol in his hand, and lodged him with Mr Boothby, of the Brick-street bridewell. Some shot and powder were also found upon the prisoner. A loaded musket was taken from another man who escaped. Mr Boothby also apprehended a woman named Mary Maxwell, who had led on the rioters to the destruction of the windows of the house of Mr Lythgoe, in Newhall-street. Amongst the offensive weapons taken, we omitted to state that there were several hammers, and that some of the bars and rods of iron weighed from 8 to 9lbs. We need scarcely add, that the females in the streets that had been assailed, were, during the whole evening, kept in a state of great anxiety and alarm,– which, indeed, no assurance of protection could allay, so much had their fears been excited by the scenes of the previous night.

Towards dusk, though vast numbers of persons continued to congregate throughout the whole length of Park-lane and St James's-street, and also at the tops of the several streets where the disturbances had taken place, it became evident the rioters would not adventure another sally; and that good humour prevailed amongst the mass of those then assembled, most of whom were drawn there from mere curiosity. Mr Whitty, nevertheless, kept his forces partly in motion and partly stationary, in Nelson-street, St James's-street, &c., until eleven o'clock.

It is impossible to form an opinion of the fatal effects which this serious riot may produce. Patrick Rice, a feeble old man, who lived in Pine-court, Crosbie-street, was struck by a carpenter with an adze with such force, that his recovery is out of the question. Several others are in a dangerous state. It is worthy of remark not a single police officer has been injured–the best compliment to their excellent organisation. Nothing, indeed, could be better than the manner in which they were marshalled. The force was broken into six divisions of fifty each, and if the rioters had not been early arrested in their movements, the consequences would have been most calamitous. We have heard, in all quarters, the highest opinion expressed of Mr Whitty's sound judgement, tact, and personal courage–qualities which were not exhibited by him for the first time. The exertions of Mr Dowling, Mr Superintendent George Tyrrell, Mr Highton, and others were most praiseworthy.

During the whole of Friday afternoon, St James's-street, and all the streets leading from it to the southern docks, bore the appearance of a town in a state of siege. The shops and houses were closed, business was suspended, and great numbers of persons were to be seen in all directions, waiting in feverish anxiety the result.

Examination of the Prisoners

On Saturday several persons were brought up at the Police-office, charged with being concerned in the riots. The Mayor presided, and the following magistrates were also on the bench:—William Brown, Esq., Robert Ellison Harvey, Esq., Francis Heywood, Esq., Charles Birch, Esq., and Richard Houghton, Esq. The Town-clerk and deputy Town-clerk were also present.

Mary Maxwell was charged by Mr Lythgoe, landlord at a tavern in Newhall-street, with having been one of a mob of persons who on Friday smashed his windows with bricks, and did much damage to his property. He went to the door to remonstrate with them, when he saw the prisoner with a half-brick in her hand. He was immediately knocked down and left for dead, but there being no evidence that the prisoner had committed any act of violence she was discharged.

Mary Burke was identified as one of a crowd of women, who, on Friday, when several carpenters' apprentices drove up to the door of Mrs Fagan's public-house, in Sparling-street,—attacked them, and threw stones after them, whereby several of the windows were broken. She was fined 10s. and costs, and in default of payment committed for eleven days.

The rest of the prisoners, namely, James Gerard, Joseph Mckenna, John Hickey Patrick Skulley, William Gallagher, John Cowan, John Gallagher, and Barney Wood were placed at the bar in a body.

Mr Dowling stated that about two o'clock on Friday last he was informed that there was a riot at the docks. He proceeded to the east side of the Salthouse Dock, when he found that the riot had been between a body of carpenters, on one side, and a body of Irishmen on the other. The parties had separated, and were at some distance from each other. He went and addressed the carpenters and they told him they would go if he would give protection to a house in Sparling-street, which was the house of Mrs Fagan. He immediately proceeded thither, and made such arrangements for the protection of the individuals inside the house, who were principally shipwrights' apprentices, as he thought necessary. Soon after this he heard a considerable noise, and, in proceeding in this direction from whence it came, he met Mr Whitty, in Wapping. There was a great commotion amongst the people, and many rumours of mischief. About four o'clock he was passing along Park-lane, with a very small body of policemen, when he encountered a body of about four hundred men, armed with staves, pikes, and bludgeons. He passed them, and met Inspector Highton with a body of men. With those he returned. The mob presented a close front, but he attacked them with his men and dispersed them. There was considerable rioting after this in many parts of the town, and, notwithstanding the exertions of the police, all the streets continued, during some time, in a state of disturbance. He (Mr Dowling) was not able to identify any of the prisoners.

Mr Whitty stated, that having heard, on the preceding day, of the rioting at the Salthouse Dock, he requested Mr Dowling to proceed thither, as he was himself exceedingly unwell, in consequence of previous exertion. A few minutes after, when he was in the Town-clerk's office, word was brought to him, that the riots were becoming more alarming, and that his presence was required. The men were just beginning to gather at the station, and he took twenty of them, six of whom were armed with cutlasses. He gave the latter orders not to draw their weapons on any account, unless they received his command to do so. He proceeded with Inspector George Tyrell to Trentham-street, where he found a great number of persons. Some of them were carpenters, many of them were much cut and bruised. The people were fleeing in all directions. The carpenters were armed with adzes, axes, and other weapons. They told him, that they would at once put up their weapons if he would give them his protection. To this he readily agreed, and having received a reinforcement of men, he directed the carpenters to fall in behind them. The carpenters gave three cheers for the police, and all proceeded together to Fagan's house, in Sparling-street, where he locked up the carpenters, and directed the armed men, whom he left in guard in front, not to allow any one to pass in or out. At the bottom of Greenland-street he met an armed mob, who showed a very dense front. They were armed with boarding-pikes and other instruments. He ordered the few armed men who were with him to draw. They rushed upon the men, who tumbled over each other, and one or two prisoners were taken. The rest were soon dispersed. As they fled, they threw down pikes, adzes, and hatchets, with which they had been armed. At this juncture Inspector Quick, with one hundred men, all of whom were armed with cutlasses, came up. He (Mr Whitty) rushed forward, and commanded them not to draw, under any circumstances whatever, without his orders. There was throughout, and for a considerable time after, great commotion in the streets. He (Mr Whitty) believed the whole disturbance originated in foolish and exaggerated reports which were circulated amongst both parties. Amongst the Irishmen it was told and believed, that the carpenters were going to pull down St Patrick's chapel, which caused the Irish to assemble from all quarters for the protection of the place of worship which they conceived was about to be destroyed. On the other hand, it was reported, amongst the carpenters, that three thousand Irishmen, who had been employed upon some railroad near Dublin, had come over to England, and having joined the Irishmen on this side the water, were about to attack the carpenters and destroy them. Nothing could be more grossly untrue than these reports.

John Gallagher was charged with having thrown bricks through the window of his house at people below; but it seemed probable, his windows having all been broken, that he was only throwing out the missiles which had been thrown in, and he was discharged.–McKenna was proved to have struck a man in the mob, and was fined 10s. and costs, or be committed for eleven days.–Hickey was proved to have behaved very outrageously in Greenland-street, throwing bricks and hurraing and instigating the mob. The prisoner was ordered to find bail for his appearance, to answer the charge at the sessions, himself in £50, and two sureties in £15 each.—Patrick Skulley for throwing bricks, which had evidently been prepared for the purpose, from an upper room, was required to give bail in £20, and two sureties in £10 each, to answer the charge at the sessions.—William Gallagher, who was armed with a bludgeon, and exceedingly violent, in Greenland-street, and James Gerard, a carpenter, were told to bail in the same amount.—John Cowan was charged with having a loaded pistol in his possession, but as it appeared that his house had been attacked, and that he was standing at his own door to defend his property from further damage, he was merely reprimanded for using so dangerous a weapon and discharged.—Barney Wood, who was proved to have been active amongst the rioters, was held to bail, himself in £20, and two sureties in £10 each.

On Monday, a carpenter, named Edward Kegan, was placed before Mr Cristopher Rawdon, on a charge of having struck a man, named Rice, with an axe, about four o'clock in the afternoon on Friday. Two or three witnesses were called, one of -

whom, an Irishwoman, distinctly swore that she saw Kegan strike Rice with an axe on the forehead. Mr Whitty mentioned, however, that although the old man had received a blow on the side of his head there was none on his forehead; and five or six carpenters were called who swore that the prisoner had been with them in a public-house during the whole of the afternoon, and did not leave their company until between eight and nine o'clock. The prisoner was discharged.

Wilful Damage.—The late Riots.—On Tuesday last, at the police-office, Thomas Lythgoe, Hugh Pugh, and John Fagan, were placed before the Magistrates, charged with having wilfully broken thirteen panes of glass belonging to the windows of John Cowan of Jordan-street.

Mr Davenport appeared on behalf of the complainant. He stated that on the 30th of May, between six and seven o'clock in the evening, a number of carpenters' apprentices assembled in Jordan-street. Amongst them were the defendants, who went to the complainant's house, and wilfully smashed his windows, breaking thirteen panes, the value of which was, as he should prove, one pound two shillings and ninepence.

John Cowan, jun., son of the complainant, was called. He stated that on the 30th May, between six and seven o'clock, he was in his father's house, in one of the upper rooms. There was a mob in the street, and, amongst the persons present, he saw the three defendants, Thomas Lythgoe, Hugh Pugh, and John Fagan. They were all throwing stones, and many of the windows were broken. Fagan threw a stone at him, but it missed him and broke the window. There were 13 panes broken altogether. He saw Lythgoe throw a stone and hit a window. There was a great mob outside, and they were all rioting.

The witness was questioned by the Magistrates as to whether he saw any of the prisoners throw stones, and these stones hit the windows. He had only seen Lythgoe throw a stone, and watched the stone hit the window. He saw the others throw stones, and heard the glass fall.

The glazier who had put in the panes was called. He said they were 1s. 9d. per pane and his bill was £1 2s. 5d.

Mr Hodgson said it had not been proved that more than one pane was broken by any of the prisoners. Fagan, it appeared, had broken one pane. He was ordered to pay 1s. 9d., or to be imprisoned five days.

Nevertheless, these early days, despite the constant possibility of local social unrest, must have given Frs Murphy, Walker and Gibson considerable personal satisfaction. The finances of the mission were on a sound footing; the interior of the chapel was transformed by the installation of an enormous oil painting above the High Altar at the front, and of a magnificent pipe organ, high up in the gallery at the back. The priests had somewhere to live; schools were opened; the mission began to play its part in the service of the local community. Soon, however, an immense challenge would have to be faced.

As its population grew from 205,974 in 1831 to 286,487 in 1841 and 376,000 in 1851, Liverpool already had one of the highest mortality rates in England, so much so that, after the 1860s, it was labelled as the 'Black Spot on the Mersey' with life expectancy at birth just nineteen years.[13]

13   C. Pooley, 'Living in Liverpool: The Modern City' in J. Belchem (Ed), *Liverpool 800 : Culture, Character and History*

In the Spring of 1847, the town was hit by a severe Typhus epidemic and also overwhelmed by large numbers of immigrants fleeing the Irish Famine (1846–52), 300,000 in 1847 alone. Many sought to continue their flight to America, but, for those who remained, there was little accommodation available to such destitute people other than overcrowded lodging houses and the filthy cellars, many of which had been closed up but were broken into. The image of one such overcrowded room provided by Wellcome Images shows an environment in which the Typhus carrying lice could spread. It also shows the challenge presented to a priest, visiting a dying person in such a room, and described by Burke: '… in the crowded rooms and cellars it was next to impossible to hear the last confession, unless the priest lay down beside the sick man to receive the seeds of disease from poisoned breaths in return for spiritual consolations. In very truth, they were braver men than ever faced the lions in a Roman amphitheatre'.[14] Gore's 'Annals of Liverpool' describes a house in Crosby Street, off Park Lane and close to St Patrick's, in which 37 people were found in one cellar; and another cellar containing eight people who had died from Typhus. In an attempt to contain the epidemic, which also included other diseases such as Smallpox and Measles, and in the face of 800 cases of Typhus in February 1847 alone, the authorities set up fever sheds in Great Homer Street and Mount Pleasant and established an isolation hospital ship, moored in the River Mersey.

The overwhelming challenge to the public health and spiritual well being of their parishioners particularly confronted the priests of St Patrick's and, indeed,

---

(Liverpool University Press, 2006), p. 173.

[14] T. Burke, *Op Cit*, p. 86.

all other ministers of religion in their area of Liverpool. For instance, in 1847, 412 victims of the fever were buried in the graveyard of the neighbouring Stanhope Street Wesleyan Methodist Chapel. During the epidemic of 1847, Fr George Gillow was a curate at St Nicholas', Hawke Street when a messenger came: 'For God's sake will some of you (priests) come to St Patrick's and bury the dead, for the church is full of corpses and the people attending them and all the priests are down with fever'. Fr Gillow went, buried the dead (he would soon afterwards bury his own brother, Fr Robert) and then went into the presbytery to find Fr Grayston dying there. A witness quoted in the 150th Souvenir History stated, 'St Patrick's Church was closed; the presbytery door stood open but there was no priest within and when Sunday came, silence reigned around the altar'.

During 1847, seven priests, based at St Patrick's, faced these challenges, with assistance from visiting clergy such as Fr John Walmesley from St Nicholas' and Fr Edmund Carter. Each of the seven is now considered in some detail.

Fr William Parker was born in 1804 and ordained at Ushaw in 1830. He came to St Patrick's in 1837 and became Senior Priest in 1841. He died of Typhus Fever on 28th April, 1847. Fifty years later, at Requiem Mass sung at St Patrick's by Bishop Whiteside for the ten Liverpool priests who died of Typhus Fever in 1847, Monsignor Nugent preached a sermon in which he referred to each of them. Of Fr Parker, he said, 'He was a man that exercised great influence in this part of the town, of a straightforward, energetic disposition, had done much for education, and the schools at that time under his direction and taught by the Christian Brothers…'.[15] For a short time, Fr Parker had the assistance of Fr Randolph Frith (1808–1893), who served at St Patrick's from October, 1842 to September, 1844.

Fr Richard Grayston was born in 1813 and ordained at Ushaw in 1840. He died of Typhus fever on 16th June, 1847, less than three weeks after Parker, from whom he had taken over as Senior Priest. Of him, Monsignor Nugent said:

> He was a model man in every sense of the word. In looks, in manner, in his tones and winning smile he exercised a powerful influence on all around him long before he was a priest. Here at St Patrick's he was adored; always at work in the church; in this densely populated district, with the old and with the young, he was a power. He was generous to a degree, all he had went to the poor, and his very clothes were given away. He caught the fever in his heroic charity by caring for the dead and placing them in their coffins when all had deserted them.

Seven days later, Grayston's fellow priest at St Patrick's, Fr James Haggar, died at the age of 29 at the house of Mr Denis Madden, 116, Islington. Perhaps he was attempting to isolate himself in north Liverpool. The fourth priest was Bernard O'Reilly, (1824–1894), from Ballybeg in County Meath, who was ordained at Ushaw on 9th May, 1847, at the age of 23, below the canonical age for ordination but necessary because of the public health emergency in Liverpool. Within a week, he arrived at St Patrick's and by June developed Typhus himself. His life was saved by Canon John Maddocks who took him out to what was then a country mission—St Oswald's, Old Swan, and nursed

---

[15] E. Goethals, *Op Cit.*

him back to health. O'Reilly returned to St Patrick's, where he remained until 1852, when he was appointed Rector of the new parish of St Vincent de Paul, in which he was consecrated as third Bishop of Liverpool in 1873 and from which he would go on to found forty two new missions and Upholland College–the Liverpool Diocesan Seminary. The saintly Canon Maddocks lived to see the opening of the magnificent Church of St Vincent, but could have had no idea of how, in saving the life of a man with so much vision as O'Reilly, he had unwittingly contributed to transformational change in the Diocese of Liverpool.

Fr James Crook, DD, (1794–1856) was appointed to St Patrick's, as Senior Priest, in July, 1847 to replace those priests who had died or departed. Born in Chorley in 1792 and ordained at Ushaw in 1818, he was a man of considerable experience, having been Prefect at Ushaw until 1824 and then successively Rector at five missions: Ashton-under-Lyne; St Augustine, Manchester; St Wilfrid, Hulme; St Alban, Blackburn and St Mary, Aughton. While at St Patrick's, he was appointed Vicar General of the diocese; he left in 1851 to become Administrator of the Pro Cathedral of St Nicholas, where he died in 1856.

Canon Crook had the support of an assistant priest, Fr Edward Kenrick, (1818–1860). Born at Hurst Green, near Stonyhurst, Kenrick was educated at the English College, Lisbon and ordained in 1842. Having worked at St Gregory, Bollington to 1845, he was transferred to St Anthony's Scotland Road, Liverpool for two years. There, he was warmly welcomed by the inspirational Fr Peter Wilcock who had spent many years in Lisbon before building St Anthony's in 1833 and was always keen to have former Lisbon students as his curates. Kenrick moved on to St Patrick's in 1847 and became Missionary Rector in 1851. He became a Canon in 1854 and remained at St Patrick's until his death in 1860. In one of his letters to Bishop Alexander Goss, he reported that the population of St Patrick's Mission had reached 13,000. A brass plaque in the church records that the fourteen Stations of the Cross in the church were erected as a tribute to him.

The Tablet, 19th May, 1860

Death of The Very Rev Edward, Canon Kenrick, Missionary Rector of Saint Patrick's, Liverpool.

This good and exemplary priest died on Wednesday, 25th April, and was buried on the following Monday at the Ford Cemetery, near to Liverpool. The clergy of the town and many from the neighbourhood of Liverpool, attended the dirge at St Patrick's Church and then proceeded to the cemetery, in company with a vast concourse of people, many of whom had come from a great distance to testify their respect for the deceased.

It is indeed strange that not a single line seems to have been sent to the 'Tablet' communicating the intelligence of his death, although three weeks have elapsed since the event.

To announce the death of a priest in a Catholic newspaper, is, in my judgment, a sure way to obtain for him the prayers of its readers. It is with this view, then, that I would ask you to insert this 'short notice' of the deceased. Canon Kenrick when a boy, was sent to the English College at Lisbon, where he passed through his course of studies for the Priesthood, with a character for gentleness and piety, that procured for him the esteem of the professors and students of that venerable institution. Soon after he was ordained, he was sent to Macclesfield, his first mission, where he

remained about eighteen months, when he was
sent to St Anthony's, at Liverpool, where he
continued to work for two years with that ardent
piety, yet unobtrusive zeal, that throughout his
missionary life had endeared him to all who knew
him. In 1847, the late Dr Brown, Bishop of Liverpool,
removed him to St Patrick's, where he remained up
to the time of his death. This year will long be
memorable for the martyrdom, by which the
priesthood of Liverpool amidst fever, and
pestilence, proved their love, and devotion, for their
flocks. There was not a church in the town that had
not to mourn the loss of some one of its pastors.
People were amazed at the calm intrepidity with
which priest after priest, in rapid succession,
sacrificed his life in attending the sick and the
dying. In the presence of such sublime acts of
charity, the virulence of bigotry for a time subsided.
Intolerance gave place to reflection and judgment,
and strangers to Catholicity and her teachings
asked each other whether it was just or honourable
to interpret the religion of such men by the
subtleties and sophistries under which it was
periodically represented at public meetings. At this
time three priests at St Patrick's had been struck
down by fever, and the graves had scarce closed
over these devoted men when the subject of this
notice entered upon his new mission. How faithfully
and with what assiduity he laboured amongst the
people, the attendance at his funeral obsequies of
nearly six thousand persons will afford some proof.
No one could be more assiduous in the discharge
of his duties. The church, the schools, and St
Elizabeth's Institute, left him scarce a moment for
the repose absolutely necessary for health. It is no
small Indication of his zeal that he should have
anticipated the Rev Dr O'Brien, in the principle on

which he has founded the Young Men's Societies, as may be seen by the working of the Young Men's Society which he has established at St Patrick's. The number of converts he received into the Church, reaching nearly a thousand, and the several religious confraternities now at St Patrick's, fully attest the character and piety of the deceased. His heart and soul were in his mission, and he succeeded, as he deserved, in all he undertook. Incidents of a public nature seldom mark the missionary life of a Catholic priest. In the narration of labours, familiar to the whole Catholic world, there are no events to startle, and no special interest to excite. Whether the Levite, whose vows are still fresh upon him, dies at the very threshold of his first mission, or his death is wept over by those whose grandsires in their childhood lisped the names of Jesus and Mary at his knees, the happiness of his people is always the motive power proposed to the priest in the great action of his ministry. Calm and innocent years, passed among poor and affectionate people, in the fulfilment of this Divine purpose, is at once, then, the simple record of his life and death. But the monument of such a man will long endure in the habits he has formed, and the lives his example has sanctified. These brief words delineate but feebly the character of Canon Kenrick, the good men he succeeded at St Patrick's are now named but seldom, and in a little while they will be altogether forgotten. And this need not surprise us, for there is a natural tendency towards oblivion common to us all, and the vicissitudes and stern realities of life only serve to confirm it. The same oblivion will soon fall upon the memory of poor Canon Kenrick, and new names and other thoughts will fill the hearts he laboured to sanctify. But while his voice is yet

> familiar to our ears, and his shadow still lingers at
> the altar he served so well, let us not fail to pray that
> God may have mercy upon him. Merciful God, grant
> eternal rest to the soul of thy servant, Edward. ONE
> WHO KNEW HIM WELL

One of Kenrick's curates was Fr Edward Walmsley who came to St Patrick's in 1850 and left to be the first Rector of the newly-formed mission of St Vincent de Paul in 1852. Tragically, he died there on 23rd November, 1852, having contracted Typhus Fever during a sick call. He was replaced there by another curate of St Patrick's—Fr Bernard O'Reilly. A third curate, at this time, was Fr Roger Arrowsmith (1823–1886) who was educated at Stonyhurst and the English College, Lisbon. Arrowsmith was curate at St Patrick's 1853–1855 but 'tensions in Liverpool so shattered his nerves that he removed to Oldcotes, Nottingham' to 1859.[16] Two other curates were Fr William Godwin (1857–1862) and Fr Honorius Magini (1859–1860). Goss refused to have Magini in his Diocese after 1860, referring, in a letter of 17th October, 1860 to 'some scandal which had been laid before him in connexion with his mission at St Patrick's'.[17]

With Canon Crook and Canon Kenrick was their assistant priest, Fr Pierse Power, who was born in 1823 and came to St Patrick's directly from his ordination in Waterford in 1847. He made a very considerable impact at St Patrick's because of what Bishop Goss termed 'his reputation of zeal and untiring energy'. Fr Power went on to become Missionary Rector at St Anthony's, Scotland Road (1859–1868), replacing the

---

16 B. Plumb, *Found Worthy* (North West Catholic History Society, 1986), p. 3.

17 P. Doyle, *The Correspondence of Alexander Goss, Bishop of Liverpool 1856-1872* (Boydell Press, 2014), p 235.

controversial Canon Thomas Newsham, and was later Rector of St John's, Kirkdale from 1871 to his death in 1895. There he built the church and continued his ministry despite blindness towards the end of his life.

As the public health crisis in Liverpool subsided and parish life assumed a more normal routine, St Patrick's was served by two rectors in the short period of eight years. The first of these was Fr Patrick Joseph Phelan who was born in Offaly in 1825 and ordained at All Hallows, Dublin in 1850. He first served in Nottingham but was moved to Liverpool in 1852 and appointed as curate at St Patrick's to assist Canon Kenrick whom he replaced as Rector in 1860. His tenure seems not entirely to have been a happy one, since in 1864 he was moved to St Anthony's as curate and retired in 1867 because of ill health. He died in 1890. Bishop Goss became severely critical of Phelan's approach to his role as Rector and wrote to him on 20th August, 1862 in exasperation:

> Some time ago, I was much pained to hear it remarked that St Patrick's had lost its old spirit, as evidenced not only by a less frequentation of the sacraments among the people, but by the manner of life among the clergy ... the clergy of the house are said frequently to spend their evenings with members of the congregation ... I hope that you will not allow St Patrick's to be considered a party house ... Discourage intercourse between your clergy and young persons of the opposite sex: I learn that young men are not always kept sober ... I hope you are pushing the matter of the new mission of Mount Carmel ... it is a cause of complaint, that whilst the

> north end is yearly founding new missions, the
> south remains comparatively inactive.[18]

It is hardly surprising that removal and demotion soon followed.

In moving to St Anthony's in 1864, Phelan would have been under the supervision of Fr Pierse Power, with whom he had served as a curate at St Patrick's. He was taking the place of Fr John Hawksworth, who was to be the new Rector at St Patrick's, and would also have met Fr Nicholas Molloy, another curate at St Anthony's who had been baptised at St Patrick's in 1832. John Hawksworth was born in Liverpool in 1829. He was educated at Ushaw and at the English College in Rome, being ordained by Cardinal Wiseman in 1853. Over eleven years, he had built up a range of experience, being curate at St Nicholas to 1855 and then St Mary, Douglas to 1857, St Alban, Liverpool to 1859 and at St Anthony's until 1864 where it was said of him 'being an excellent musician, he trained the choir there'. In 1868, he became curate at St Augustine, Preston and from 1872 until his death in 1888, he was Rector of St Mary, Chorley.

Fr Hawksworth had taken up his appointment as Rector of St Patrick's in November, 1864. After the scandals surrounding his predecessor, he would have been welcomed by a young curate who had come to St Patrick's in September, 1863, fresh from ordination and who would remain at St Patrick's for 58 years–Fr Edward Goethals. When Hawksworth left, Goethals became Missionary Rector, and St Patrick's entered an unprecedented period of stability and firm leadership.

---

[18]   P. Doyle, *Ibid*, p. 289.

7 The Typhus Epidemic of 1847

I T HAS BEEN calculated that, during 1847, the population of Liverpool increased by 137,519 as a result of people fleeing from Ireland during the Famine.[19] Their overcrowded and insanitary accommodation contributed to the spread of Typhus, from which 21,000 died in that year alone.[20] The epidemic prompted the following letter from a prominent local surgeon:

Liverpool Mercury, Tuesday, 29th June, 1847

Fever in Liverpool

To the Editors of the Liverpool Mercury

Gentlemen,

Whilst the Select Vestry are frittering away their time in useless contentions and neglecting the responsible trust reposed in them, fever is progressing with giant strides. So formidable, indeed, has become the evil, and so malignant the disease, that there are just grounds for fearing that Liverpool is to become the Skibbereen of England.[21]

Giving the members of the Select Vestry credit for the best of intentions, I cannot but consider the means they have adopted to be worse than useless; for they have lulled the public into a false belief that they were meeting the exigencies of the case, which, in reality, they were not.

---

[19] T. Burke, *Op Cit*, p.84.
[20] E. Midwinter, *Old Liverpool* (David and Charles, 1971), p.84.
[21] The region around Skibbereen experienced a significant famine in the years 1845–52, a time referred to as The Great Hunger.

When we bear in mind that in Liverpool there are at present upwards of 8,000 cases of fever, and most of these are in the most densely populated, the worst ventilated, and the most filthy parts of the town—(localities at all times the hot-beds of fever)—when we bear in mind that in these localities fever has attained a malignancy and infectiousness equalled only by the Plague,—when we bear in mind, also, our comparatively paltry fever hospital accommodation,—we are forced to fear that as yet we are but entering on the scene of desolation that lies before us.

Hitherto, this pestilence has selected its victims from the most destitute and most helpless of our over-crowded population—from amongst the Catholic clergy, nearly over half of whom have laid down their lives in administering the consolations of religion in the fetid and poisonous atmosphere of crammed cellars and garrets,—from amongst medical men, who have braved danger and death in their efforts to administer to suffering humanity,—from amongst the ill-paid and over-worked benevolent parish officers;—but now, infection-like, the deadly poison has begun to diffuse itself amongst the middle classes of society, many of whom are being bemoaned by their bereaved relatives.

Hear then, ye more favoured and more wealthy of the community: the gaunt disease is at your doors and unless immediate and ample accommodation be made for the reception of those already stricken by the pestilence, it will know no distinction of rank in its victims. Let, then, every man who values his own life, who values the life of his wife or his child, speak to the Select Vestry in a voice that cannot be misunderstood, and urge, and if need be, compel them to more efficient means.

The time, then, has arrived when it becomes us to throw aside all squeamish and ill-judged decency as to the fear of creating alarm in the minds of the timorous; the truth must be spoken aloud, it is already spoken from the graves of our departed friends. Interested considerations of trade now no longer availing, all fastidious but mistaken parish economy, must now give way to the dictates of real humanity and self preservation.

Let, then, the Select Vestry bestir themselves in a body, and endeavour to eradicate the source of the evil by establishing receptacles for 6,000 fever patients in the outskirts of the town; let them remove each infested individual from the sinks of filth and disease before he has contaminated those around him; thus, and thus only, will they be able to stem the torrent which is sweeping before it the lives of hundreds, the peace of mind of thousands, and the domestic trade of Liverpool.

Yours &c.,

W. T. Callon, Surgeon

13, Islington.

At the beginning of 1847, Liverpool had 24 Catholic priests; by the end of the year, 10 had died of Typhus contracted when ministering to the dying. They were:

Fr Peter Nightingale of St Anthony's, 2nd March.

Fr William Parker of St Patrick's, 27th April.

Fr Thomas Kelly, DD, of St Joseph's, 1st May.

Fr James Appleton, DD OSB, of St Peter's, 26th May.

Fr John Austin Gilbert, OSB, of St Mary's, 31st May.

Fr Richard Grayston of St Patrick's, 16th June.

Fr James Haggar of St Patrick's, 23rd June.

Fr William Vincent Dale, OSB, of St Mary's, 26th June.

Fr Robert Gillow, of St Nicholas's, 22nd August.

Fr John Fielding Whitaker, of St Joseph's, 18th September.

Despite this huge loss, it should not be forgotten that death from Typhus was a constant hazard for Catholic priests in Liverpool, in the mid nineteenth century. Fr Thomas Leonard of Soho Street, for instance, died on 25th September, 1848 of 'Malignant Typhus' and was buried in the vaults at St Anthony's.

St Patrick's lost more priests to Typhus in 1847 than any other Liverpool parish, so it is fitting that all ten 'Martyr Priests' are commemorated by a Celtic cross erected in front of the church. It was solemnly blessed by Bishop Whiteside on Sunday, 2nd October, 1898 and cost £145. The ten priests are also commemorated in silhouette in a widely circulated print.

8 CANON EDWARD GOETHALS
1868–1921

ROM THE DAY of its opening, the priests serving St Patrick's were aware of, and drawn into, a series of issues which contributed to the extremely volatile nature of the local community. One, Fr Roger Arrowsmith, had had to withdraw from St Patrick's in 1855 because tensions in Liverpool 'shattered his nerves'.

Tensions existed between Irish and British Catholics; between rich and poor; between Free Traders and Protectionists; between immigrants and locals competing for employment; between Tories and Liberals on the Town Council; over voting rights; the teaching of religion in schools; British and Irish politics; church building; workhouse provision and public health to name but a few. Underlying all was the constant fear of mob violence which frequently burst out into the open. Liverpool might have been a port of international significance; but it was also a very inward looking town where local issues often proved to be violently controversial.

Bishop Goss's action in appointing Edward Goethals to St Patrick's was an enlightened and far sighted move. Coming from Belgium, Goethals approached each issue with an open mind; he could not be seen as British or Irish, Tory or Liberal; he had a broader and more impartial view.

Edward Goethals was born in Eccloo, Belgium, on 20th July, 1840, educated at the Seminaries of Ghent and Bruges and ordained on 23rd August, 1863.

Appointed to St Patrick's in that year, he remained
there throughout his priestly life, progressively becoming Missionary Rector, Canon and Dean. He would
have understood one issue at St Patrick's very well,
having survived Typhus as a young priest. His hand
can be seen in the History of 1911 ('Gleanings') to
which reference has already been made. Brian Plumb
says of him that he lived to become one of the most
respected clergymen on Merseyside.[22]

The Archives of the Archdiocese of Liverpool preserve a very large scrap book in which Canon Goethals
pasted letters, illustrations and press cuttings, recording the history of St Patrick's Parish and issues with
which he was involved; it provided him with a context
for the actions which he took and helps us to see them
through his eyes.

Turning the pages of the scrap book, we can see St
Patrick's taking the lead in encouraging Catholics to
vote, with the inauguration of the Catholic Registration
Society held at St Patrick's schoolroom in July, 1839.
We see Liverpool Corporation establishing elementary
schools as early as 1826, but, with the Tories in control
of the Corporation from 1841 to 1892, their policy
excluded Catholic children, leading Catholic parishes
to found their own schools. By 1844, St Patrick's
Schools had over 1,000 children on roll.[23] The system
they established would only be changed by Forster's
Education Act of 1870. The official Blue Book of that
year showed that, in Liverpool, only 6,202 Catholic
children, out of a possible 20,000 were attending
school; but the reality was not so much a shortage of
school places but more the extreme poverty of many

22   B. Plumb, *Op Cit*, p. 57.
23   T. Burke, *Op Cit*, p. 76.

families who relied on the earnings of relatively young children. Goethals would have recognised the irony in the establishment of a branch of the Health of Towns Association in Liverpool at St Patrick's in 1846.

In another place, he would have seen how the political controversy over the Act of Union of 1801, leading to disputes between Unionists and Repealers had, in 1841, led his predecessor, Fr Parker, to forbid the placing on the church doors of a petition to Parliament demanding that the Act of Union be repealed. Despite receiving support from Daniel O'Connell, MP, Parker was accused of being 'anti-Irish' by some members of his congregation, a dispute which Burke says 'had the effect of severing the Irish and English Catholics (of Liverpool) from working harmoniously'.[24] When knowledge of this dispute became widely known, local Catholics were accused of working to destroy the union between Great Britain and Ireland; a mob marched from Toxteth and broke up an Anti-Corn Law League meeting in Great George's Place and then moved on to smash the windows in St Patrick's Chapel and its school. Burke records how 'the wife of a policeman was saying her prayers quietly in the church when the infuriated mob made the attack and, as a consequence, lost her life from fright, an incident which increased animosity on both sides'.[25] Feelings ran high and, the next day, the windows of the nearby Anglican Church of St James were smashed in retaliation, despite Parker's appeal against revenge. This may be one reason why Parker asked for the St Patrick's Day parade of 1845 to be abandoned. Controversy over St Patrick's Day parades became particularly strident

---

[24]   T. Burke, *Op Cit*, p. 67.
[25]   *Ibid.*

in the early months of 1847 and was vividly recorded in the correspondence columns of the *Liverpool Mercury*. Goethals could not have failed to see the irony that Parker, the priest at the centre of the controversy, died on 27th April, 1847 when the Typhus Epidemic temporarily eclipsed the bitterness of the disagreement.

> Some years ago, the Rev William Parker very insultingly kicked from the vestibule of St Patrick's Chapel a table on which lay a petition for the restoration of Ireland's Parliament. The reverend and respected clergymen (and none more deservedly so) of the other districts did not interfere. Mr Parker was the only politician amongst them, and although he not only permitted but encouraged the signing of petitions on other subjects, he refused to allow a petition for a repeal of the Union to lie for signature at the door of the temple reared by the sweat of the brow and the labour of the hands of Irishmen. In the following March, the deputies of the different Hibernian societies met in committee, over which that venerable and ever beloved clergyman, Mr Wilcox, presided, for the purpose of making arrangements for St Patrick's Day. It was decided by a large majority that the societies would not go that year to any church with which Mr Parker was connected, and St Anthony's was selected. Mr Parker, who was in attendance on the committee, *immediately* left, and from that period dates his animosity towards the whole body; the chapels have since that time been closed against them. This year the committee decided by a large majority *not to walk in procession* unless a chapel was opened and a sermon preached. Three of their body were accordingly selected to wait on the Right Rev Dr Brown. We now publish the correspondence, and leave it to the Catholic public to say, whether men who placed themselves at the feet of their Bishop

have not been most undeservedly, and, in violation of all etiquette, most contumeliously treated, and whether the charge of deception made against those who waited on the Bishop by Mr Parker, and reiterated by the Right Rev Dr Sharples on last Sunday, be correct or not. While we beg respectfully to give it as our opinion that the display of last Sunday, instead of adding to the dignity of the Episcopacy, must tarnish the lustre of the mitre; yet we acquit his lordship of intention to insult, being firmly convinced he would not have made the charges he did, were it not for erroneous impressions, made on his mind by the foulest calumnies and the grossest misrepresentations. No insult was offered to Mr Parker by any man in the procession. The story about £200 being spent in sashes and colours is so ridiculous, as scarcely to be deemed worthy of an answer. *It is well known* that those sashes and flags have been in our possession for years. We are pained, deeply pained, for the sake of our common faith and holy religion, to be compelled to appear in print. The course adopted towards us leaves no alternative; and we rest satisfied that, when the whole is calmly considered, no blame can be attached to the members of the Hibernian Societies, and no honest Catholic, however scrupulous, but will acquit them of any intention of disrespect towards their bishops and clergy.

To the Right Rev Dr Brown

MY LORD—On the part of the officers and members of the different Hibernian societies, we beg, respectfully, to address your Lordship. We have had a general meeting for the purpose of considering the best manner in which we could celebrate the approaching festival of our national saint. The extreme distress in Ireland caused us to adopt the following course, *subject to your*

Lordship's approval:- That we go in procession to some of the Catholic Chapels to attend the holy sacrifice of the Mass and to hear a charity sermon preached on the famine. That each man, before joining this procession, pay a certain sum, and promise to contribute as much as his means will permit at the sermon. It is not, we can assure your Lordship, to indulge any party feeling or make any tawdry display, but we really believe a sum of money will be thus raised, which as far as it goes, will alleviate the wants and mitigate the sufferings of our afflicted and distressed countrymen.

We beg to subscribe ourselves, with great respect.

Your Lordship's most obedient, humble servants.

Denis Arkwright

Timothy Crowley

Mathew Gahagan

Liverpool, 9th March, 1847

Was there any deception practised here? After the lapse of three days, we received, through the Rev Mr Newsham, the following reply:—

Bishop Eton, February 12, 1847

Dear Sir—Be so good as to inform Mathew Gahagan, 79, Richmond-row, that the benefit societies may have their charity sermon at St Anne's, about which they made application—I remain, dear Sir, very truly yours,

+ G Brown

To the Rev Thomas Newsham

Is there any man in his senses can doubt taking the above letter as an answer to the foregoing one, that this was a full and unqualified permission to walk?

The letter of the Right Rev Dr Brown, read off the altars, and already published in the papers, came next, calling on the different clergymen to discountenance a procession, as he understood, men, calling themselves Catholics, intended holding one; we wrote the following letter to his lordship.

My Lord—On last Sunday a letter was read from the different altars in Liverpool, addressed by your Lordship to the respective clergymen of each district, intimating your Lordship's wish that no procession of Irishmen should take place on St Patrick's Day. We do not mean to dispute your Lordship's right to do so; but as the different Hibernian Societies, which were presented when we waited on your Lordship, are placed in an awkward position before the public, we feel it due to you and ourselves to publish the conversation we had with your Lordship, and the letters that passed between your Lordship and ourselves, in order to vindicate our own characters before the public, and show clearly that in all our proceedings we have been actuated by the purest motives. When we waited on your Lordship at Bishop Eaton, before you invited us into your sitting-room, you desired to know whether we were connected in any way with the United Order of Catholic Brethren, as you could not countenance any deputation from them, on the ground, as your lordship alleged, that they had acted irreligiously and deceitfully towards your Lordship, using your predecessor's name by misrepresentation, and your Lordship's name without your sanction, and as they were to use your Lordship's own words a 'worse species of Freemasonry,' a body, in fact, that your Lordship would feel it your duty to denounce from every altar in your Lordship's district. Your Lordship will remember that we expressed no opinion one way or other, respecting our Catholic brethren, save and except that we were not connected with them. Being assured of this fact, and that we represented no societies having secret sign or password, your Lordship politely invited us in, and entered on the subject of our mission. The letter we handed to your Lordship fully explained our object, and your Lordship and the public must see by it that our great anxiety was to *do nothing contrary to your Lordship's wishes*. In fact, we urged a gentleman to accompany us who, before he consented to do so, exacted a promise from us, that whether your Lordship directed a Church to be opened for us or not, whether your Lordship sanctioned a procession or not, we should strictly adhere to your Lordship's injunctions. Your Lordship, after taking two days to consider the matter, sent us a letter of sanction. Guess, then, our surprise at hearing your Lordship's letter read on Sunday last, designating us, 'men who called themselves Catholics.' Had your Lordship communicated with us—had your Lordship written a single line to say you had re-considered the subject and changed your mind, we should have no cause for complaint; but that your Lordship felt it your duty to denounce men anxious to comply with your Lordship's wishes, and to pronounce them on a most important point, their soul's salvation, public liars strikes us with great astonishment. We understand that statements have been made to your Lordship describing us differently from what we represented ourselves. If so, my Lord, we do not hesitate in giving such statement the attest contradiction, and solemnly declare that we withheld nothing from your Lordship, and that in all we said we were not guilty of a single untruth. My Lord, we are Catholics, not in name, but in reality, the possessors of the religion of the sainted martyrs of old, and our persecuted forefathers we pride in as our brightest inheritance. We are Catholics, my Lord, because we have been taught and believe that we belong to the church built upon the rock, against which the storms may rage, the tempests howl, the billows foam, and the waves dash round its sides, but cannot shake its firmness. We are Catholics, my Lord, because it is our fixed and solemn conviction that as long as we place unlimited faith in the doctrines of our church, implicit confidence in its dogmas, are guided by its counsels, and influenced by its example, the souls which the great God, our Maker, gave us in trust will remain in '"immortal youth" unhurt amidst the war of elements, the wreck of matter, and the crash of worlds.' We are, my Lord, attached to our religion, not, my Lord, because it is fashionable, but because it is true.

Trusting that we have, in this vindication, satisfied all right-thinking men that we have done no wrong, and sincerely hoping that, in the explanation which we have felt it necessary to give, we have not been in the slightest degree disrespectful to your Lordship,

We beg to subscribe ourselves,

With great respect, your Lordship's obedient, humble servants,

Denis Arkwright

Timothy Crowley

Mathew Gahagan

Liverpool, 22nd February, 1847

The Rev Mr Brewer's Reply

Dear—The Bishop wishes the festival of St Patrick to be celebrated at St Anne's with all solemnity on the feast of the saint. We shall, therefore, be prepared to sing a solemn high mass, preach a sermon for the destitute brethren of our holy faith in Ireland, on the 17th, and the only part of the arrangement which disappoints the wishes of the Bishop is the *street procession*, which the timid mind of your kind Bishop fears may lead to a breach of the peace.

I remain, my dear sir, yours, faithfully,

Henry Brewer

St Anne's, Edge-Hill, March 4th, 1847

Does his Lordship in this letter forbid the procession? Certainly not. He did subsequently, when all preparations were made for it; and in order to pay to his Lordship and the reverend gentleman who kindly officiated on the occasion the greatest possible respect, the men walked quietly to the church of St Anne, left it in the same manner, and formed their procession afterwards. Not a single inebriated man was to be found amongst them during the whole day; no money was spent in dinners or drink, and they returned to their respective domiciles as quietly as when they left them in the morning.

Denis Arkwright

Timothy Crowley

Mathew Gahagan

As a child of eight, Goethals would probably have retained some memories of 1848, a year when there was political revolution in many European countries, leading, for instance, to the third French Revolution. In Britain, the politicians were fearful of an uprising in Ireland, and, in Liverpool, the authorities were so concerned that they enrolled 3,000 special constables to prevent anticipated civil unrest on St Patrick's Day. Fr Bernard O'Reilly of St Patrick's publicly condemned political insurrection, but he still had to lead his people to defend the church from determined attacks by Orangemen, whose objective was to pull down the statue of St Patrick from its place, high up on the west wall of the church. Ladders and ropes were used, bitter street fighting ensued, and the mob eventually departed, having only broken one finger off the statue.

Goethals would have discovered a recent difficulty in the burial of the dead. By 1859, out of Liverpool's estimated population of 460,000, 150,000 were Catholic and space for further burials in vaults or graveyards such as those at St Patrick's was rapidly becoming scarce.[26] Then, in response to the Typhus and Cholera epidemics, the Intra-Mural Act of 1859 forbade the burial of any further human remains within town boundaries. Canon Thomas Newsham of St Anthony's responded to this problem by purchasing 24 acres of land from the Earl of Sefton at Ford, where a new Catholic cemetery was inaugurated on Sunday, 22nd September, 1859 with a procession from St Patrick's to Ford, led by Bishop Goss. The *Liverpool Mercury* reported that 'several hundred carriages, cabs, omnibuses and spring carts, laden with passengers, drove behind the bishop's carriage'.

Goethals would have read that, although Fr Kenrick had estimated the population of St Patrick's to be 13,000 towards the end of his incumbency in 1860, the average Sunday attendance had been calculated in 1855 by Nathaniel Cowie to be only 7,632.

The response which Goethals made to this seemingly overwhelming series of inter related problems was both uncompromising and straightforward. He would do all in his power to foster the faith of his people, defend their interests and uphold the law of

---

[26]   T. Burke, *Op Cit*, p.150.

the land at all times. This can be seen in the following five examples.

In February, 1870, two years after having become Missionary Rector, he devised a successful plan to build a new, additional school for girls and infants in Hyslop Street, behind his presbytery. By 1878, the new church of Our Lady of Mount Carmel had been opened, to serve the southern end of his parish, followed by St Bernard's in 1901 and St Malachy's in 1904. In 1880, after years of tense negotiations, he was successful in having a Catholic chaplain appointed, for the first time, to the Smithdown Road Workhouse (later Smithdown Road General Hospital, a site occupied in 2020 by ASDA). This person was his curate, Fr James Fanning, who came to St Patrick's in 1878 and held the post of chaplain — and that of chaplain to the Little Sisters of the Poor in Aigburth — until his death on 10th September, 1909. From 1897, Goethals assisted Monsignor James Nugent in establishing a home for unmarried mothers and their children in South Liverpool, to be run by the Sisters of the Sacred Hearts of Jesus and Mary. Canon John Bennett indicates that the House of Providence was first based in a mansion located in west Dingle but later moved to 'Kelton' in Woodlands Road, Aigburth.[27] Finally, we can hear from Goethals directly, writing in response to a report in the *Liverpool Courier*. First, two differing accounts are given of the same meeting, one taken from the *Liverpool Mercury*, the second from the *Liverpool Courier*, followed by three letters in response to the second article, the second letter being from Fr Goethals. The date is July, 1886.

---

[27]   Canon J. Bennett, *Fr Nugent of Liverpool* (Liverpool: CCPS, 1949), p. 121.

Meeting of Orangemen

A public meeting, which was called by handbills addressed to the 'Loyal and Law-abiding' citizens of Toxteth-park, was held last evening in the Nelson Hall, Mill-street, 'to consider what means should be taken to suppress the rowdyism and lawlessness that now disgrace this part of the city.' Brother Jones presided and there was a large attendance ... In opening the proceedings, the chairman said it was a well-known fact that Toxteth-park during the past week had disgraced itself. The City Council had taken notice of the matter, and Dr Commins had referred to the windows being broken of a Roman Catholic place of worship. He must remind them that the windows of five or six Protestant places of worship had also been broken. (Hear, hear.) He referred to the damage done to these half dozen chapels, &c and said it was simply a sample of the lawlessness of the Roman Catholics. It had been said that the disturbances arose from Orange bands parading the streets. This he denied, but at the same time he was not in favour of them going out so much. Having spoken of the duties of Orangemen, he said that the Roman Catholics might take these bands as an insult, but it was not intended as such. (Applause.) He called upon the Orangemen to give up a little and show that they did not intend to bring disgrace upon their order. (Hear, hear.) In doing so, the Roman Catholics would see that it was not the Orange party who were leading in this matter. He asked them to curtail their liberties. Last year he had to seek protection at the Essex-street Bridewell, and this year he had to stand at his door until a certain body of men passed by, or his windows would be broken. ('Shame'.) He could only say, even in the presence of the reporters, that if his windows were again broken, it would be a 'hospital case'. (Applause.) He would not stand it; he was not prepared to give up his rights as a citizen. (Hear, hear.) If the authorities would not take steps to put this lawlessness down, they must take steps themselves. They ought to form some such society as the 'Knights of Freedom'. They would know each other; take districts to patrol like policemen and thus put down all lawlessness. (Applause.) There certainly were some rowdies on their side and they were a disgrace to them. They should be looked after as well as the Catholic rowdies. (Hear, hear.) ... The policemen were overworked, and many of them stood by and watched windows smashed because they dared not touch the offenders.

Bro Davies next addressed the meeting. He said that 18 years ago nobody was an Orangeman unless he got drunk and beat his wife; but things had now changed. (Hear, hear.) Although it had been said that both 'Orange and Green' took part in these disturbances, yet it was a fact that in nine cases out of ten, the Orange party was the party attacked. (Hear, hear.) ...

Bro Houston moved that 'a letter be sent to the authorities demanding that they should take steps at once to put down the disturbances' ...

The Liverpool Courier

The Faction Disturbances at The South End: An Orange Protest

A public meeting of the 'loyal and law-abiding' citizens of Toxteth-park was held in the Nelson Hall, Mill Street, last evening, to consider, as the circular convening the meeting stated, 'what means should be taken to suppress the rowdyism and lawlessness that now disgrace this part of the city.' There was a large attendance and the utmost unanimity prevailed throughout the proceedings. Bro T. Jones (Master of the Orange Lodge No 612), who presided, said it was a well known fact that during the past weeks Toxteth-park had been disgraced by the rowdyism which had been prevalent. He quite agreed with the statement by Dr Commins, made in the City Council on the previous day, that adequate measures were not taken by the police authorities to cope with the existing lawlessness; but he denied the assertion of the learned doctor that Roman Catholics and Roman Catholic places of worship had suffered by the disturbances. (Applause.) He was prepared to prove that the bell of St Patrick's Chapel rang at 23 minutes past ten on Sunday night, and it was evidently done by some pre-concerted arrangement, because immediately afterwards mobs of Irish men and women rushed along Park-place shouting, 'To the Chapel!' No danger could possibly have been apprehended to the chapel and the bell seemed to have been rung with the object of creating disorder by alarming the Irish population of the neighbourhood. Windows at the back of the chapel were broken on Friday night, but he had learned that this was not done by members of the Orange bands, but by a number of Irish women who were carrying stones in their aprons. Mr Paull, speaking in the Council, complained of 49 squares of glass being broken in a Roman Catholic chapel, but if Mr Paull had taken the trouble to make inquiries, he would have found that many Protestant places of worship had been damaged in a similar way. Windows had been smashed in the church schools, St James-road; in the Tabernacle; the Methodist Chapel, Park-place; the Hyslop-street Mission-hall; St Matthew's Church, Hill-street; St Barnabas Schools and Holy Trinity Church, Parliament-street. These were a few examples of the lawlessness of the Roman Catholic party. (Applause.) He was not in favour of the Orange bands parading the streets quite as extensively as they had hitherto done but he emphatically denied that the recent disturbances had arisen from that cause. The windows of his house had been threatened to such an extent that he had been obliged to apply for police protection, but his appeals had been in vain. If, however, anyone attempted to break his windows, he would assure them it would be a hospital case. (Applause.)

...

Orange Protest Against Rowdyism

To the Editor of the *Liverpool Courier*

Sir,

In your report of the above meeting you say that I had applied for police protection in vain. Will you please correct this? What I did say was that both last year, and the year before, I had to apply for police protection to prevent any damage being done I cannot do otherwise than to bear my testimony that the police try to do their duty in a manner to earn the respect of all law-abiding citizens, and as one I can sympathise with them in their efforts and trust that all such will rally to their support if required. I am &c.

Liverpool, 9 July 1886 T. Jones

To the Editor of the *Liverpool Courier*

Sir,

During these days of excitement, the bell of St Patrick's has been rung for the services of the church at the usual hours, and at no other hours. Brother Jones says that he is prepared to prove that it was rung at 23 minutes past 10 o'clock on Sunday night. All I can say is, that if Brother Jones can prove that, I shall look upon him as a wonderfully clever brother.

I think your readers will agree with me that, notwithstanding the brother's good intentions, his speech will not tend much to suppress the rowdyism and lawlessness of which he so justly complains. Yours &c.

22, Park Place Edw. Goethals

To the Editor of the *Liverpool Courier*

Sir,

Toxteth-park is in a great state of turmoil at present owing to party feeling in connection with the elections, and considerable damage has been done to various places of worship since last Friday by gangs of lawless persons, and there threatens to be more damage done, as there are no signs of the bitter feelings subsiding, but the contrary. The commencement and main support of all this animosity seems to be the parading of various bands and processions playing party tunes &c., and it is quite time they were stopped.

Has not our chief constable power to do this, both legally and physically? If not, he should have it at once, and use it impartially and firmly, for, if something is not immediately done, there will, I fear, be scenes enacted between now and Monday next that are new to Liverpool, culminating that day in a regular riot.

It would be far better and cheaper in the end, for a number of special constables to be sworn in if necessary, than for the ratepayers to have to pay for the damage that will in all probability be done. Yours &c.

July 9, 1886 PEACE

The immediate context of these reports and letters is the imminent Orange Lodge celebrations, due on July 12th and made more complicated by controversies arising from recent elections.

Perhaps one of the most important events in St Patrick's Parish during the incumbency of Canon Goethals was the Golden Jubilee of the opening of the church. This was celebrated on Monday, 2nd September, 1877 and was reported in both the local and the national press.

The *Liverpool Mercury* of 5th September, 1877 provided a detailed description of the way the church had been decorated to welcome Cardinal Manning, followed by a detailed summary of his sermon:

> The fiftieth anniversary of the opening of the Roman Catholic Church of St Patrick, Park Place, was celebrated yesterday. The exterior of the sacred edifice bore fitting indications of the event. At the main front entrance on the right hand side was a shield bearing the inscription 'Welcome to his Eminence Cardinal Manning' and another on the left bore the words 'Welcome to his Lordship the Bishop of Liverpool'. Under the conspicuous statue of the saint, whose name the church bears, was the Pope's coat of arms, while on shields and banners interspersed around the walls were represented St Patrick of Ireland, St Augustine of England and St Andrew of Scotland, with the following mottoes: 'God bless our land', 'God save England', 'Hail to Saint Andrew the herald of the cross'. Flags were flying representing the Papal colours, on which were the words 'God bless our Pope' and above all was the emblematic flag of St Patrick. At High Mass ... the musical portion of the service was entirely Gregorian, the choir being a voluntary one,

> composed solely of male voices, under the
> conductorship of Mr Vollen ...

Comparing this with the music for the opening of the church shows how much the music for great liturgical occasions had changed in fifty years.

Canon Goethals had pasted into his scrap book a cutting from a national (Catholic?) newspaper but its name is not included. This report concentrates more on the liturgy inside the church before again giving a detailed summary of Cardinal Manning's words.

> On Sunday last, the golden jubilee of St Patrick's Church, Park-place, Liverpool was celebrated with especial grandeur. His Eminence the Cardinal Archbishop of Westminster preached during the forenoon service, when the Right Rev Dr O'Reilly, Lord Bishop of Liverpool celebrated Solemn High Mass ... About twelve months ago, the Church was entirely re-painted and decorated by Messrs Jelley and Hughes of Slater- street, Liverpool. In anticipation of the visit of his Eminence the Cardinal, the roof has been a second time painted and regilt by the same firm, and the whole interior of the sacred edifice presented a pleasing and tasteful appearance. The altar ornaments were elaborate and chaste, and on the front of the side and central galleries were affixed scrolls bearing the names of various deceased clergymen who had in their lifetime been connected with St Patrick's. Several other scrolls were displayed, which bore expressions of affection and welcome to his Eminence and his Lordship the Bishop ... At the High Mass, his Eminence the Cardinal was assisted by the Rev J. Hegarty as presbyter assistant; by the Revs P. Flynn and J. Norris as deacons to the throne and by the Rev

> Father Green, sub-deacon, as crossbearer. His
> Lordship the Bishop was assisted by Frs Krebs
> and Goethals as presbyter assistant and deacon
> of the Mass. Fr Sullivan officiated as sub-deacon
> and the Rev Dr Sommer as crossbearer. The Rev
> W. Spencer was Master of Ceremonies ...[28]

The Cardinal's text was 'So speak you and so do, as
being to be judged by the law of liberty'. He spoke of
reasons for celebrating the fact that the church was fifty
years old. It had been opened when Penal Laws were
still in force; 'the most cruel legislation the world had
ever seen'—but those 'laws against the holy faith of
Jesus' Church' had now been repealed and Catholics
were free to practise their faith. Fifty years ago, the
church in England had no Hierarchy, but now it had.
St Patrick had brought the Catholic faith to Ireland and
the Irish had taken it all over the world. 'In the great
Council of the Vatican, when the Catholic Church met
together by representation, there was no one saint or
apostle that had in that august assembly so many
mitred sons as the Apostle of Ireland. That was the
reward that God gave to those who served Him in the
law of liberty'.

From 1863 to 1921, Canon Goethals was at the very
centre of the life of St Patrick's parish, guiding it from
the aftermath of the Typhus epidemics through the
American Civil War, the first Vatican Council, the two
Boer Wars, the Easter Rebellion in Ireland and the First
World War. He came to Liverpool when quill pens and

---

[28] Fr William Spencer became the first Rector of St Clare's,
      Sefton Park and died in 1892 while chasing a man who had
      robbed an offertory box at his church. Dr Dagobert Sommer
      had been Secretary to the Archbishop of Cologne but was
      exiled from Germany during the Kulturkampf and was curate
      at Our Lady of Mount Carmel 1877–1884.

horse drawn carriages were commonplace; when he died, they were being replaced by telephones and motor vehicles. His commemorative stone can be seen in the wall of the Memorial Hall and School, built in 1927, facing the church in Park Place, the scale of the building perhaps representing the enormous esteem in which he was held. This is also made clear in the following tribute, written anonymously in 1923 referring to this new building.

> February the 23rd was a sad day in the history of St Patrick's. The Canon lay dead, and his people bereft and inconsolable stood in the streets and in their houses bowed in prayer while from the old belfry the mournful news was tolled far and wide. In that day of grief were crowded poignant memories of wondrous charity, of burning zeal, of rare, devoted service—all of those golden bonds, alas! now broken, that bind the Catholic pastor to his flock and make him the beloved Father of his people. Time has tempered that sorrow, but has not lessened the gratitude of his children, which is the inspiration of the gigantic effort they are now making that his memory may not fail.
>
> Sixty years have passed since Father Edward Goethals came to St Patrick's a young curate and exile from his native town of Ecloo in Belgium; and, until death closed his eyes at the great age of 82, faithfully did he spend himself in God's service. His motto ever was 'Ora et Labora', Prayer and Work—unceasing prayer for his children and the spread of God's Kingdom—untiring zeal for the founding of new missions and the building of new schools.

The churches of Our Lady of Mount Carmel and St Bernard, and latterly that of St Malachy, the schools in South Chester Street, Hyslop Street and Robertson Street, and in some measure many of the missions erected the city during the last fifty years, all speak of his zealous labours before the burden of years and of suffering bade him rest.

Annals of the Young Men's Society, The Holy Family, the Children of Mary, the Propagation of the Faith, the St Vincent de Paul Society, tell of his care for the older members of his congregation. In each and all of these organisations (which he founded in the parish) his influence was powerful enough to make them pre-eminent at one time or another in this great archdiocese and all still survive vigorous and beneficient memorials of his zeal. Three great virtues set their seal on all his labours and made them fruitful: his charity, his simplicity and his humility.

It was his extraordinary charity that bound him so closely to his people. Ever anxious to conceal his innumerable benevolences, no effort of this kind could hide from them his gentleness towards the wayward, his tenderness and solicitude for the poor, the aged and the infirm, and the practical succour he so surely discovered and applied to their relief. Simple as a child himself, he dearly loved the little ones, delighting in their company, sharing their joys and sorrows, and sparing no effort to safeguard their innocence and confirm their faith. Gladly he suffered them to come unto him, and this early affection was rewarded a hundredfold by life-long love and reverence which it inspired.

Not less remarkable than his simplicity of character and abounding charity was his great humility. To be esteemed the least among the brethren and to remain the humble parish priest was his most ardent desire; and though he appreciated the dignity of the title 'Dean' and 'Canon' the bestowal of these honours brought him no joy fitting to compensate for the loss of the name 'Father' in which he gloried.

For the glory of God and the salvation of souls he lived and laboured, leaving to his brethren a sublime example of unworldliness and zeal, to his people a legacy of charity expressed in glorious and fruitful work—to all, the memory of a wonderful life nobly spent in the grandest of all callings.

His nephew, Fr Alphonse van Wassenhove offered the Requiem Mass which was attended by the entire Chapter of Liverpool. Metropolitan pro-Cathedral; the crowded congregation included the Rev J. Bell-Cox, Vicar of the Anglican Parish Church of St Margaret, Princes Road.

A different tribute was described in St Patrick's School Log Book:

28th February, 1921 … Children taken to Park Place at 11.30 to pay last homage to our beloved Rector, Father Edward Canon Goethals as he was borne to his resting place in Ford. The Canon died 23rd February 1921. RIP.

The Canon would probably have smiled to see a Log Book entry written just over two weeks later:

17th March, 1921 … The Rev M. Timmons, M.A., the new Rector, paid his first visit to the schools.

> He gave sweets to the children in honour of the
> feast of St Patrick.

Canon Goethals' gravestone at Ford Cemetery is an exact copy of the 1898 Celtic cross in front of St Patrick's Church, commemorating the ten Catholic priests who died in Liverpool in the 1847 Typhus epidemic.

9 FR MICHAEL J. TIMMONS MA, 1921–1928

ICHAEL TIMMONS WAS born in Co. Meath in 1873 and ordained for the Liverpool Diocese in 1902 by Bishop Whiteside. An academic, he spent fourteen years as a seminary professor before serving as curate and then parish priest in Newton-le-Willows 1916–1921. His incumbency as Parish Priest of St Patrick's was short—he died in office after only seven years in 1928.

Three issues dominated these seven years, the second and third being inter-related. The first concerned Mr Jack Traynor (1883–1943) whose faith impressed Fr Timmons so much that he encouraged Jack, against the advice of his doctors, fellow priests and even his wife to join the Liverpool Archdiocesan Pilgrimage to Lourdes in 1923, led by Archbishop Keating.

Jack Traynor was educated at St Patrick's School; he was so severely wounded in the First World War that his legs were paralysed, his right arm atrophied, he was epileptic and had a hole in his skull closed with a silver plate. He was discharged from the armed services, officially classified as permanently and completely disabled and confined to a wheel-chair, his emaciated body covered with pressure sores. Despite all opposition, he insisted on making the journey by train to Lourdes where, after bathing in the water and receiving a blessing during the procession, he found that all his injuries had disappeared. The news caused a sensation, particularly when three doctors certified that the cure had taken place and could not be explained by medical science. On the return train journey, Archbishop Keating approached him and Jack knelt down to receive his blessing. In his own words, 'He (the archbishop) raised me up, saying, 'John, I think I should be getting your blessing ... do you realise that you have been miraculously cured by the Blessed Virgin?' When his train reached Lime Street Station, crowds of people stampeded to see him. He returned home, established a successful coal and haulage business, and returned to Lourdes every year as a helper. As a form of thanksgiving, Jack financed two Lourdes grottoes, one at St Malachy's, the other at St Patrick's. The latter has now disappeared, but it stood facing inwards towards the North portico, against the wall overlooking North Hill Street. As part of the bi-centenary plans, a replacement grotto of Our Lady of Lourdes is planned, with a plaque to commemorate Jack's astonishing cure. His death, in 1943, was unconnected with any of his wartime injuries. In view of its successful outcome, Fr Timmons received considerable credit for the advice he had given to Jack. Kelly's (Gore's) Directory of Liverpool for 1933 contains the following entry: Traynor, John, Coal Merchant, 121, Grafton Street and Cartage Contractor, 149, Grafton Street: Telephone Royal 1923.

The two other issues concerned the Centenary of the opening of St Patrick's Church and the acute shortage of School accommodation in the parish. Regarding the latter, while there were 2,000 children of school age in the parish, permanent accommodation was only available for 1,000. Thus, on 8th May, 1921, an appeal was launched for the Canon Goethals Memorial School Fund, with a target of £19,000. This was further developed by the organisation of a great bazaar at St George's Hall in March 1923 with an executive committee led by three members of the City Council, including Peter Kavanagh still commemorated in the local public house which bears his name. The laying of the foundation stone of the new school by Archbishop Keating on 21st August, 1927 was seen as the chief feature of the Centenary celebrations. The scale of the school can be seen from the capacity of its first floor assembly hall—1,800 children; the building was designed for community use also. Simultaneously, an additional new school was built in Jenner Street, behind the church, opened by Bishop John Barrett, an old boy of St Patrick's, on Sunday, 1st May, 1927.

The Centenary of the church was celebrated with Pontifical High Mass at 11 am on Sunday, 21st August, 1927, in the presence of Archbishop Keating. The *St Patrick's Centenary Souvenir Programme* provides the following details of the proceedings:

> Celebrant: The Rt Rev J. Barrett, Bishop-Auxiliary of Birmingham.
>
> Deacon: The Rev A. W. Madden, Curate, St Patrick's.
>
> Sub-deacon: The Rev J. J. McLaughlin, Curate, St Patrick's.
>
> Assistant Priests: Very Rev Canon O'Sullivan, Curate at St Patrick's 1875–1878; Rt Rev Mgr O'Brien, DCL.
>
> Assistants at the throne: The Rev J. Myler; The Rev J. Kelly.
>
> Master of Ceremonies: The Rev J. Wareing, Archbishop's Secretary.
>
> Preacher: Rev J. Howard.
>
> The afternoon programme included a public procession at 2.30 pm; the laying of the foundation

stone of the new schools at 4 pm; and Pontifical Benediction at 6.30 pm, the preacher again being the Rev J. Howard. Interestingly, Fr Timmons is not mentioned, although his successor as parish priest was deacon at the Mass. He died on 5th November, 1928.

The celebrations continued on the Monday with a Solemn Requiem Mass for deceased priests of St Patrick's and an evening concert in the Picton Hall; and, on the Thursday, there was a children's picnic in Ainsdale.

10 Canon Arthur Madden VF, 1928–1942

A RTHUR MADDEN WAS born in Bootle in 1885. Following education at Upholland, he was ordained in 1912; became Dean in 1931 and Canon in 1938. Over a period of thirteen years, he served as curate at the pro-Cathedral; St Sylvester; English Martyrs', Preston; St Patrick, Wigan and St Hugh, Liverpool. He came to St Patrick's in 1925 as curate and became Parish Priest there from 1928 until his death from peritonitis on 23rd January, 1942.

He served as Chaplain to the Liverpool Catholic Cemetery Board but his main responsibility, with curates such as Frs Henry Moffatt, Patrick Monagle, Felix O'Hagan and Francis McHardy was to care for the needs of a parish of 10,000 souls in a deprived, dockland setting. During the Second World War, bombing raids necessitated the closure of the parish schools and the evacuation of the children for two years, from 15th September, 1939 to 18th August, 1941.

His Requiem Mass was celebrated by Canon William Daly of Holy Cross, St Helens in the presence of Archbishop Downey and attended by over seventy priests. The sermon was preached by his friend, Fr Joseph Dickinson who had been ordained with him in 1912.

When Fr Madden first came to St Patrick's in 1925, with its population of 10,000 + parishioners, it might have taken him quite some time to encounter a 14-year old boy who had been a member of the parish scout group, who lived alone with his Irish mother, and who had an unusual name: William Patrick Hitler. By the time of Madden's death, in 1942, he would certainly have been aware of this young man.

In 1910, Alois Hitler, a waiter at the Shelbourne Hotel in Dublin, whose half-brother was the then little-known Adolf Hitler, had met a young woman called Bridget Elizabeth Dowling. The lovers eloped to London, where they married at Marylebone on 3rd June, 1910 and subsequently settled at 102 Upper Stanhope Street, Liverpool, in St Patrick's parish, where their son, William Patrick Hitler, was born on 12th March, 1911, and subsequently baptised at St Patrick's Church.

Alois Hitler established various businesses in Liverpool: a restaurant in Dale Street; a boarding house in Parliament Street; and an hotel in Mount Pleasant. Having become bankrupt in 1913, he fled to Germany to elude his creditors, subsequently joined the German army, and married bigamously. Later, he encouraged his son, William Patrick, to travel to Germany, which he did in 1929. After his half-uncle Adolf Hitler became Chancellor of Germany in 1933, William Patrick was able to exploit his family connections to secure a senior position at the Reichskreditbank in Berlin, and subsequently with Opel Motors. Refusing an invitation to renounce his British citizenship in 1938, and sensing personal danger, he returned to live with his mother in Liverpool and wrote an article for *Look Magazine* of 4th July, 1939, entitled 'Why I Hate My Uncle'. That year, he moved with his mother to the United States and joined the US Navy Medical Corps on 6th March, 1944, following a special request to President Franklin D. Roosevelt. He was wounded in action and awarded the Purple Heart. Having left the navy in 1947, he worked as a laboratory technician and eventually established a blood analysis business. He also changed his surname to Stuart-Houston, and, following his marriage to the German Phyllis Jean-Jacques, had four sons, none of whom had children. He died on 14th July, 1987, and is buried alongside his mother (who died in 1969, aged 78) at the Holy Sepulchre Catholic Cemetery, Long Island. Ironically, the house at 102 Upper Stanhope Street, was destroyed in the last German air raid on Liverpool in 1942.

11 MONSIGNOR LAURENCE CURRY, 1942–1975

AURENCE CURRY WAS born in 1902, in Lodge Lane, close to St Patrick's. Appropriately, he was ordained by Bishop Barrett on 2nd June, 1928. He became a Privy Chamberlain in October, 1942; Dean in 1947; and was Archbishop Heenan's first appointment as Canon in 1957. Having spent a short time after ordination as curate at St Joseph's, Liverpool, he went to the Beda College in Rome, at the end of 1928, to study Canon Law at the Gregorian University. He was recalled to Liverpool in 1929 to become secretary to Archbishop Downey 1929–1942. He was Parish Priest of St Patrick's for 33 years from 1942 to his sudden death on 23rd September, 1975 in Paradise Street, Liverpool.

Monsignor George Mooney recalls his time at St Patrick's as a young priest. He recalls a way of life many aspects of which his contemporaries would have experienced, including the dominant authority of the parish priest and the housekeeper.

> In September, 1956, I arrived at St Patrick's to be the junior curate of four with Monsignor Curry, P.P. The parish was large and very busy, consisting of old type tenements and older terrace houses. The population was virtually all white working class, with most of the men dockers. The presbytery was an old, three storey terrace house on the opposite side of Park Place from the church. There was one combined bathroom and toilet for five priests.

I never did discover what the arrangements were for the Housekeeper (who was Fr Paddy Doran's aunt) and the three Irish maids. There were several parish schools. My memory of them is not very detailed since I worked in the Curial Offices every morning, in the Marriage Tribunal, and had little to do with the schools. There were four public Masses every day and the fifth priest celebrated on a side altar—long before the days of concelebration. We were also chaplains to the Royal Southern Hospital—long since gone. Sundays were hectic: after Mass and an early breakfast, we went out on the outdoor collection, complete with a runner who went on ahead, warning the next house of the imminent arrival of the priest and incidentally giving the man of the house time to disappear if he wasn't a Mass goer. We also collected at all the public houses where a pint glass would be passed around. Then came baptisms. There was no preparation required—whoever turned up was baptised, and most Sundays a small army would arrive. There was also Sunday School and finally we had a meal in the late afternoon. No evening Mass, of course, but Rosary, Sermon and Benediction. All marriages were on a Saturday afternoon. It could be a hair raising experience since Monsignor Curry booked all weddings for 2.30 pm, which meant some weeks more than one party arrived at the same time. The ensuing chaos can be imagined. The huge church demanded good lungs for a preacher at Mass since this was before the days of microphones. I was put in charge of the Catholic Men's Society and managed to per-suade Monsignor to let me install a bar in the club—a first, I think in the South end—but certainly not the last. I spent four very happy years at St Pat's. My departure was unusual, to say the least. I was deputed to go to the Cathedral crypt to act as subdeacon to Archbishop Heenan's Christmas Midnight Mass in 1959. At the end of the Mass, the Archbishop called me over and, at 1 am on Christmas morning, he told me he was moving me to Atlantic House as assistant port chaplain. I duly left St Patrick's in January, 1960 to take up my new appointment — but that's another story.

Monsignor Cyril Taylor was a close friend of Monsignor Curry and, like him, had served as secretary to Archbishop Downey. He was a regular contributor to the 'Catholic Pictorial', 1962–1978. That his reputation as a powerful orator was well deserved can be seen from his words at Monsignor Curry's funeral on 30th September, 1975:

Once before I was privileged to speak in this church. It was February, 1967, when I was asked to preach at a Mass of Thanksgiving for the silver jubilee of the parish priest. Everything then was light and joy. Today an almost impenetrable gloom has descended on the parish of St Patrick and upon the episcopate and clergy of all ranks and ages in the Archdiocese. Of course, we know that there is light beyond the gloom and maybe the one we mourn is already happiest of all because his mode and manner of life left him little to fear from the judgment.

Laurence Frederick Curry was a Liverpudlian belonging to the Sefton Park area, and Providence decreed that his entire priestly life, save one year, should be cast within walking distance of his natal place. Through St Edward's

College and Upholland he went to Oscott, where he was ordained on 2nd June, 1928, the eve of his twenty-fifth birthday. The ordaining bishop was Dr Barrett, the auxiliary of Birmingham, who was born and baptised in this parish. Of the fifteen priests ordained on that day, which included the future Bishop Bright, only four remain, and only one in our diocese: Canon Thomas Kennedy, happily with us today. Father Curry was appointed curate at St Joseph's, Grosvenor Street, but his stay there was short. Dr Downey became Archbishop in August of that year and selected him to go to Rome to read Canon Law at the Gregorian University, but recalled him a year later to be his second secretary. Those were halcyon days for the Catholic body, beginning with the great education demonstrations in anticipation of the 1929 Parliamentary elections, followed by the massive gathering at Thingwall Park to celebrate the centenary of Emancipation, which drew a crowd of 400,000 people, the largest assembly of Catholics in this country since the Pilgrimage of Grace; then Brownlow Hill site was purchased in the teeth of opposition, and Lutyens' cathedral scheme was launched. As one of the Press corps who covered these events and who attended the Tuesday morning briefings at Archbishop's House, I met Fr Curry frequently. He was placid and imperturbable, kind and considerate, constant and helpful to a degree. He had an infectious laugh usually accompanied by a vigorous rubbing of the hands. He seemed immune to moods; something changeless in a changing world. He never broke a confidence nor a friendship and the denial of a request by him was almost like a concession.

In 1931 I was one of forty lay people who accepted an invitation to meet Mr Frank Duff at the Good Shepherd Convent, Wavertree. This led to the formation of the first praesidium of the Legion of Mary in Liverpool itself, and the first ever mixed praesidium in the world. Father Curry became spiritual director and remained so for thirty years until the work he set us to do, visiting the hovels and hostels of St Joseph's parish, became redundant through slum clearance and the advent of the Welfare State. But he retained his active connection with the Legion of Mary, and his interest continued until last week.

When I joined the Archbishop's staff in 1939, I was able to observe at closer range the life style of this exceptional priest. In addition to our curial duties the secretaries served as chaplains to the Good Shepherd Convent, Eton Lodge, Woolton Road, Wavertree where the Community Mass was at ten past six in the morning in pre-war days. Fr Curry couldn't even ride a bike, much less drive a car, and the walking time was 25 minutes. For the best part of 13 years, he footslogged to the convent in all weathers. He never complained and was never late. His large bed-sitting room at the top of the house, in Woolton, occupied a gable end and had two massive windows. There was no central heating and it could be perishingly cold, but only in the worst of conditions did he allow himself the luxury of a one bar electric fire. He rose at five o'clock and washed and shaved in cold water from a ewer and basin. His first commitment every day, wherever he might be, was his morning meditation. He kept the fasting laws of Lent, Advent and the Ember days, when they applied, with a couple of extra days prescribed for tertiaries, rigorously but inconspicuously. I was never in his room at Woolton or Park Place but a lamp was burning before a statue of Our Lady. The rosary, litany and spiritual reading were part of the routine, and Lourdes an annual event. Sometimes we said office in choir.

Although he lived increasingly in the presence of God and was punctilious in all his duties, he loved his fellow man, bore no ill-will and never lost the human touch. He agonised over many of the changes in the Church, and, while tardy in implementing some, he never protested. But this ordered and hidden life enhanced rather than militated against a natural gaiety, which made him an acceptable table and holiday companion. Nevertheless, he had a legalistic and enquiring mind with a stubborn streak, which could dismay a casual acquaintance and aggravate those who knew him better. He was tenacious of his own opinions, but more often than not was tantalisingly right. Hence you will know with what fiendish delight I was able to point out to him an omission from his recent panegyric on Father Anderton. It evoked a hearty laugh.

This, then, was the man around whose mortal remains we are gathered to pay our last respects and make suffrage for his soul. The key-note of his virtuous life was utter devotion to duty. Who of us would break off a holiday to attend a prize giving we had witnessed thirty times before?

Your Grace (Archbishop Beck), in the three dioceses you have been called upon to serve, you can have had no finer or more dedicated servant, and we, his colleagues in the cloth, no grander example of priestly virtue.

My Lord Mayor, we appreciate your presence here this morning, and we know your own sense of personal loss, with the added poignancy that Monsignor Curry was to have preached at your Civic Visit to St Clare's. Our sympathy, likewise, goes out to his family and many friends, to his orphaned parishioners, his staff and especially Miss Doran, who retired early this year, after being 33 years in his service and even longer at St Patrick's presbytery.

And now we say farewell, but be assured of this, if there is laughter in Heaven, Monsignor Curry will see as much humour as tragedy in receiving the final call in the heart of the city he loved in a street called PARADISE!

12 FR THOMAS LYNCH, 1975–1977

HOMAS LYNCH WAS born on 17th January, 1923 in Co. Roscommon. His parents were James Lynch and Mary K. Browne who had a business in Main Street, Ballinlough, to which his brother-in-law, Peadar Keaveney (2020) remembers him returning twice each year when he was serving as a priest in the Liverpool Archdiocese. He had two brothers and five sisters. Thomas Lynch was educated at St Jarlath's College, Tuam, and later at St Patrick's, Carlow, where he was ordained on June 5th, 1949. On arrival in Liverpool, he was Curate at Holy Trinity, Garston to 1951; then at St Brigid, Liverpool to 1960; St Patrick, Southport to 1961; St Edmund, Waterloo to 1966; and Our Lady of Walsingham to 1972.

In 1972, he joined Monsignor Curry at St Patrick's as curate, and succeeded him as Parish Priest in 1975. He was making plans for the 150th Anniversary of the church when he became ill and died in the nearby Royal Southern Hospital on 27th August, 1977 after a short illness.

The choice of hymns at his Requiem Mass reflects both his own character and the liturgical tastes of the time:

Entrance: All Ye Who Seek A Comfort Sure.

Kyrie: Plainsong Mass for the Dead.

Offertory: All That I Am.

Sanctus: Plainsong.

Agnus Dei: Plainsong.

Communion: Oh, Jesus Christ Remember; Christ Be Beside Me.

In Paradisum: Plainsong

Recessional: Alleluia, Sing To Jesus.

Fr Gerald McCusker, in 2020, Parish Priest of St Mary's, Euxton, was curate at St Patrick's in 1977, having been appointed there to assist Monsignor Curry and then Fr Lynch when he succeeded as Parish Priest. He looked after Fr Lynch during his final illness. He remembers the shock of arriving at inner city St Patrick's from the suburban parish of Christ the King, Childwall.

> Monsignor Curry was a wonderful pastor, loved by his parishioners ... I knew Tom Lynch from my home parish of St Edmund's, Waterloo. Both of us are Irish, him from the South and I from the North, and we got on well together. He had a great sense of humour, and a loud, gruff voice. A big man, he was dedicated to the parish and to the Southern Hospital. A man's man. Easy to talk to ... I remember the night he died in the Southern Hospital and I was called out ... People could not believe it, he was a very popular priest ... Oh, I really loved the people and remember their lovely, strong faith.

A more formal tribute appeared in the *Catholic Pictorial* in September, 1977:

> The second parish priest of St Patrick's, Liverpool to die within two years was buried last week. Fr Thomas Lynch, who took over the Toxteth parish from Mgr Lawrence Curry in October, 1975, was 54.
>
> He was taken ill while making a sick call at the Southern Hospital a few weeks ago. After feeling a pain in his chest Fr Lynch went along to the Casualty Ward, from where he was admitted to the hospital.

Fr Lynch was born in Ballinlough, Co. Roscommon, and educated at St Jarlath's College, Tuam. He studied for the priesthood at St Patrick's, Carlow, and was ordained in 1949.

After a short time in Birmingham Fr Lynch came to Holy Trinity parish, Garston, where he served as assistant priest until 1951. He spent the next nine years at St Brigid's, Bevington Bush, before moving to St Patrick's, Southport.

In 1961 Fr Lynch was appointed to St Edmund of Canterbury, Waterloo, where he served for five years. He first came to St Patrick's, Liverpool, as assistant priest in 1972, after six years at Our Lady of Walsingham parish, Netherton.

In his sermon preached at the Requiem Mass on Wednesday Archbishop Worlock said that Fr Lynch had come to know and love the people of St Patrick's, and to be with them in a way which showed his confident understanding and patient faith in their future.

'When he became ill a few weeks ago, the prayers, the good wishes, the concern of his people, their constant efforts to break through the protective cordon in the Southern Hospital—all of these things were a sign of the very great extent to which the parishioners here had come to accept and love Mgr Curry's successor in these last years,' said the Archbishop.

'They had found a strong man, a gentle but dependable giant, whose rumbling gruff voice could not disguise a full and understanding heart.

'In the hard times through which this historic parish has been passing in recent years, the care of St Patrick's has inevitably been—even from its very geography—an uphill task. But so was the road to Calvary, and the reward was the same.

'Fr Lynch was a well-known and unchanging figure as he moved through the streets here, undeterred by falling numbers and demolition, anxious only to attend to the spiritual needs of those who remained to give them heart and to sustain their faith.

'And we who remain must go on: in the same spirit of humble, unquestioning and obedient faith: confident in the future, and in the meantime working together in the service of God and of our neighbour.'

After the Requiem at St Patrick's, Fr Lynch's body was taken to Ballinlough for burial. The interment was attended by Bishop Gray and a number of priests from the southern deanery of the inner city.

Emer Keaveney Ray, his niece, wrote about him on 6th January, 2021, from her home in Spain, first referring to her mother, Terry, Fr Lynch's sister:

They were very close siblings, and his death was a terrible suffering for her. She often remarked that his favourite hymn was 'Nearer my God to Thee' and it was that hymn that was sung as he left the church of his childhood in Ballinlough to be buried in the church grounds, one of only four graves there, all occupied by former priests … As a child of 8 years, Uncle Tommie's death was my first experience of real sadness and death, indelibly etched in my mind. He had been a regular visitor to us, and was much loved by adults and children alike for his sense of fun and generous nature. Everton was his team and he was quick to tell my mother that we should be dressed in blue and white—certainly NOT in red and white!

13 FR JOSEPH MARSH, 1977–1981

OSEPH MARSH WAS born on 25th November, 1929 in Chorley and was ordained at Upholland on 26th May, 1956. He served as curate at St Clare's, St Malachy's and St Michael's, Liverpool; then at St Marie's, Widnes, Our Lady of Compassion, Formby and St Cuthbert's, Pemberton. In September, 1977 he succeeded Fr Lynch as Parish Priest of St Patrick's, moving in 1981, after only four years, to St Agnes, Huyton; in 1993 he became Parish Priest of Our Lady, Help of Christians, Tarleton, from which he retired in 2006 and died the following year in Southport. He was the first parish priest of St Patrick's not to have a curate: the population of the parish had fallen to 4,500.

In 1978, the 150th Anniversary of the church was celebrated with a series of Masses:

> Wednesday, 15th March, 1978: Concelebrated Mass with Bishop Augustine Harris and priests of the Deanery, 7.30 pm.
>
> Thursday, 16th March, 1978: Concelebrated Mass with Bishop Joseph Gray and priests who had served at St Patrick's, 7.30 pm.
>
> Friday, 17th March, 1978: Concelebrated Mass with Archbishop Derek Worlock and priests who had attended school at or lived in the parish, 7.30 pm.
>
> Sunday, 19th March, 1978: Civic Mass in the presence of the Lord Mayor of Liverpool, Councillor Paul Orr.

In response to a request from Fr Lynch, Anthony J. Hocter produced an illustrated history and brochure to commemorate the anniversary.

Born in 1961, and having grown up in St Patrick's parish, where he was an altar server, Mark Hughes entered St Joseph's College, Upholland in 1973 to try his vocation for the priesthood. Now, in 2021, a funeral director in Liverpool, and looking back on the period 1974–1978, Mark vividly remembers two episodes in the history of the parish. The first is of the earthquake in Bala, North Wales which took place on 23rd January, 1974. Its effects were so widespread that they had an impact on Liverpool where they were thought to have caused the total collapse of the house immediately next door to the presbytery whose inhabitants, including Fr McCusker, were severely shocked. Fortunately, their home was not badly damaged.

Mark's other memory is of the seminary's requirement that, during vacations, students were discouraged from staying with their parents; the recommendation was that they should stay at the presbytery of their home parish. Mark's room was on the top floor of 22 Park Place, next to the tank room from which the sounds of plumbing in the house were a constant presence. The top floor also afforded a good view of the West front of the church, across the road, and of the unusual inhabitant of the church crypt. Joseph was from Jamaica and, for some years, with the blessing of the clergy, and unconcerned about the adjacent burial vaults, he lived in the large space at the front of the crypt where he slept in a bed he had constructed himself. Invariably clad in trilby hat, shirt, tie and braces, Joseph could be seen hanging washing on his line in the church grounds or busy with his primus stove, watching potatoes boil as he sat on his stool. He was also regularly supplied with meals carried across Park Place from the presbytery by Miss

Doran and, later, Mary Brown, successive housekeep-
ers. His presence afforded an unusual level of security,
his candles shining far into the night. By day, he could
be seen hoeing the grounds, waving to passers-by.
Suddenly, he was no longer there. He had quietly
removed his belongings and left a farewell note, found
by Larry Foy, the church caretaker and Martha White,
the sacristan. Joseph was never seen again.

14 CANON LEO STOKER, 1981–1998

ANON LEO STOKER's period as Parish Priest of St Patrick's almost exactly coincided with the period when Derek Worlock was Archbishop of Liverpool, 1976–1996. It was a difficult time, but also, perhaps, a turning point in the fortunes of St Patrick's.

Liverpool was particularly badly affected by the national recession in the 1970s and 1980s. Unemployment grew rapidly, politics became radicalised, the population decreased, there was rioting in the streets. A vivid symbol of the Toxteth Riots of 1981 was the burnt out shell of the Rialto Cinema, the twin domes of which overlooked St Patrick's parish. Another vivid symbol of decreasing population and declining religious practice can be seen in the closure of at least nine large churches, all bordering on Toxteth and within walking distance of St Patrick's. These included Mount Zion Chapel, Princes Avenue, destroyed by fire in 1973; Princes Gate Baptist Church, abandoned and vandalised, 1974; All Saints, Bentley Road, demolished, 1974; Trinity Presbyterian Church, Upper Warwick Street, demolished 1974; The Wesley Methodist Chapel, Upper Stanhope Street, demolished 1970; Sefton Park Presbyterian Church, Brompton Avenue, demolished 1975; St Paul's, Princes Park, demolished 1976; The Welsh Presbyterian Church, closed 1982, neglected, then abandoned, now roofless; and St James, Upper Parliament Street, closed in 1974, but reopened in 2010, after 36 years. A later (1994) determined attempt to have the neighbouring church of St Vincent de Paul closed was ultimately unsuccessful.

In his book *The Worlock Archive*, Clifford Longley explores some of the factors underlying the Toxteth Riots. While, in 1981, Worlock refers to the 'phenomenon of alienation' which seemed to be behind the social unrest in Liverpool, at the time of the riots, and a serious breakdown in police and community relations, Dennis Norman and George Erdos, emphasise the 'collapse of the inner-city working-class culture of family life, primarily focused on the domestic redundancy of males'.[29]

It is perhaps a tribute to the tenacity of Fr Stoker and the community he led that St Patrick's parish survived intact throughout this period of social deprivation. Its relative decline may perhaps be measured in the statistics of enrolment of children for primary education at St Patrick's, taken from the Liverpool Archdiocesan Directories: 471 in 1979 and 297 in 1998—a creditable achievement, given that the official population of the parish had fallen by 50% from 4,000 in 1979 to 2,000 in 1998.

The brutally radical reordering of the sanctuary at St Patrick's, which took place during Fr Stoker's incumbency, is covered in a separate chapter. 'Some things will have to be changed to bring the church into line with liturgical requirements', he told the 'Catholic Pictorial' on 16th March, 1986. Major adjustments would have to be made around the High Altar. 'No decisions have been made about this as yet, but it will have to go. An effective sanctuary will have to be made there. At present the marble altar is preceded by a flight of steps which are of no practical value liturgically speaking and simply taking up space which could be better utilised'.

---

[29]   C. Longley, *The Worlock Archive* (London: Chapman, 2000), p. 335.

Slater's design for the interior of St Patrick's was one where each individual component complemented all the others, with attention focused on the sanctuary from every part of the church. Its removal would destroy this concept, its replacement incompatible with the character of the overall building, compromising the integrated scheme and saving hardly any space Nevertheless, the new scheme went forward and, on Friday, 3rd December, 1993 Archbishop Derek Worlock led a concelebrated evening Mass of Rededication, in which the new altar was blessed and the restored Crucifixion altarpiece revealed. In its report of 12th December, the Catholic Pictorial reported the archbishop's comments about how the dilapidated condition of the church in the late 1970s reflected the problems then facing the local community: 'challenging circumstances … bulldozers, apathy, dispersal and local politics'. He had given Fr Stoker a slogan to work to: 'A Restored Church; Renewed Worship and the Old Faith', and felt that his confidence in the parish priest had been justified by what he saw around him.

Ill health prompted Fr Stoker's move, in 1998, to the parish of Corpus Christi, Rainford, from which he retired in 2019.

15 FR PATRICK FOLEY SPS, 1998–2002
FR KENNY HYDE, 2002–2008
FR JOHN SOUTHWORTH, 2008–2018

HIS TWENTY YEAR period has been one where St Patrick's has been served by priests who have also had varying responsibilities in the neighbouring parishes of St Vincent de Paul, Our Lady of Mount Carmel and St Malachy's, all of which were founded from St Patrick's, as was St Bernard's which was closed in 2012 and eventually converted into low cost accommodation. St Malachy's was closed in 2001 and subsequently demolished. Since 2015, St Patrick's and Our Lady of Mount Carmel have been merged into one parish, with the parish priest living at Mount Carmel presbytery. The priests' house, which served St Patrick's throughout almost the entire time when it was an independent parish, has been converted into apartments; and the Canon Goethals Memorial Hall and School has likewise been sold. Local traditions have significantly diminished—a good example being the annual Orange Lodge parades on 12th July, once such a prominent feature in different parts of north and south Liverpool.

From the early 1990s, the centre of Liverpool has been progressively redeveloped, particularly in terms of new hotels, apartment blocks, leisure facilities, educational initiatives and student accommodation, especially in the formerly redundant dock areas. New museums have opened, celebrating the history and heritage of Liverpool, culminating, perhaps, in the city being chosen as European Capital of Culture 2008. By 2018, this progressive regeneration had reached the borders of St Patrick's parish, Parliament Street and the South Docks; the proposed reopening of the railway station at St James's Place, closed in 1917 after a serious accident some years before may be a sign of regeneration moving directly into the parish in years to come, bringing with it new employment opportunities, expanding from the Baltic Triangle.

Officially, the population of the parish has been remarkably consistent during this period: 2,000 people every year from 2001 to 2016; the number of children attending the primary school declined from 287 in 2001 to 134 in 2010. A year after Fr Southworth's arrival the number had increased to 174 in 2011 and reached 205 in 2015.

Fr Patsy Foley is a member of the Kiltegan Fathers, a man of wide pastoral experience, including as port chaplain, an extrovert with a pragmatic, energetic approach. Fr Kenny Hyde was ordained by Archbishop Worlock in July 1995 at Our Lady of Mount Carmel Church. He was the first man from Toxteth to have become a priest for many years, the first known being Thomas Molloy who was baptised at St Patrick's in 1832 and ordained in 1858. Like him, Kenny Hyde has a good understanding of the St Patrick's community.

Fr John Southworth spent many years as parish priest of St Michael's Ditton, where, as at St Patrick's and Mount Carmel, he was able quietly to pursue his profound interest in organ music. His leadership was gentle, purposeful and collaborative. When he left St Patrick's in 2018, to become parish priest of St Paul's, West Derby, he deposited, at the Archives of the

Archdiocese of Liverpool, a complete set of the news-letters of the parish, produced during his incumbency — an enormously valuable insight for future historians on the day to day workings of this poor, inner city parish in its response to the issues surrounding it.

16 FR SILVIU CLIMENT, 2018-

FR SILVIU CLIMENT brings to the parish of St Patrick and Our Lady of Mount Carmel pastoral experience obtained both in Romania and in Italy, and thus a broad outlook not unlike that of Canon Goethals. His energy and enthusiasm have already seen Mount Carmel church comprehensively redecorated; the organ at St Patrick's rehabilitated and brought back into regular use; and comprehensive plans for the restoration of St Patrick's church in which the rediscovery of its original lease may have its part to play. The restoration will include rehabilitation of the interior and, as such, will mirror the restoration of the nearby Church of St James, now reopened after having been closed for thirty six years, and also work on the neglected graveyard of Wesley's Chapel, the third of those three churches which mark the growth of organised Christianity in the South of Liverpool at the turn of the eighteenth and nineteenth centuries. Fr Silviu is confident in leading the parish to face the opportunities and challenges ahead. In this work, he will have the collaborative assistance of the four, recently arrived Missionaries of Africa at the neighbouring and newly-prospering parish of St Vincent de Paul: Fr Ferdinand van Campen; Fr Terry Madden; Fr Charles Obanya; and Cardinal Michael Fitzgerald, thus preserving the link established when St Vincent's was founded from St Patrick's in 1852.

17 St Patrick's Presbytery

22 PARK PLACE, LIVERPOOL 8

THIS HOUSE, FACING the church, and with its distinctive balcony above the fanlight, seems to have been the residence of the priests serving St Patrick's almost from the beginning until comparatively recently. The Census of England and Wales gives some details of its inhabitants.

Household	Role	Sex	Age	Birthplace
1841				
William Parker	Priest	Male	35	Lancashire
George Gibson	Priest	Male	30	Lancashire
Richard Grayston	Priest	Male	25	
Ann Pennant	Servant	Female	30	
Alice Much	Servant	Female	20	Lancashire
Mary Woods	Servant	Female	15	Lancashire
1851				
James Crook	Head	Male	57	Chorley
Edward Kendrick	Inmate	Male	32	Hurst Green
Bernard O'Reilly	Inmate	Male	27	Ireland
Pierce Power	Inmate	Male	27	Ireland
Hanna Pennant	Servant	Female	43	Sutton, Cheshire
Catherine Pennant	Servant	Female	24	Stowey, Cheshire
Sarah A Price	Servant	Female	17	Liverpool, Stouting
Helen Livarbrick	Servant	Female	25	Richest, Lancashire

Household	Role	Sex	Age	Birthplace
1861				
Patrick J Phelan	Head	Male	37	Ireland
William Godwin	1st Curate	Male	40	Liverpool, Lancashire
James Singleton	2nd Curate	Male	30	Liverpool, Lancashire
Henry H O'Bryan	3rd Curate	Male	27	Montpellier
Elizabeth Bonney	Housekeeper	Female	45	Wigan, Lancashire
Jane Greyson	Housemaid	Female	20	Liverpool
1871				
Edward Goethals	Head	Male	30	Belgium
Patrick Flynn	Curate	Male	29	Ireland
Julia Blake	Servant	Female	30	Ireland
Bridget Conway	Servant	Female	22	Ireland
Ellen Wynne	Servant	Female	21	Ireland
1881				
Edward Goethals	Head	Male	40	Belgium
Michael Rea	Boarder	Male	28	Ireland
James Fanning	Boarder	Male	23	Ireland
John Hanley	Boarder	Male	24	Ireland
Ann Hudson	Servant	Female	42	Ireland
Elinor Salisbury	Servant	Female	25	Liverpool
Mary Gerard	Servant	Female	16	Liverpool
1891				
Edward Goethals	Head	Male	50	Belgium
Edward O'Reilly	Boarder	Male	31	Ireland
James Smith	Boarder	Male	28	Lancashire
Joseph Buchanan	Boarder	Male	25	Lancashire
Ann Hudson	Servant	Female	48	Ireland
Helena Hudson	Servant	Female	20	Lancashire
Ann Olphert	Servant	Female	42	Ireland

Household	Role	Sex	Age	Birthplace
1901 31ˢᵗ March				
Edward Goethals	Head	Male	60	Belgium
William H Byrne	Assistant	Male	60	Dublin
Patrick Lynch	Assistant	Male	28	Longford, Ire.
James O'Dwyer	Assistant	Male	25	Limerick, Ire.
Jane Gregson	Housekeeper	Female	60	Liverpool
Elizabeth Hayes	Servant	Female	20	Liverpool
Mary Pickarvance	Servant	Female	18	Liverpool
1911				
Edward Goethals	Head	Male	70	Belgium
Patrick Lynch	Boarder	Male	39	Longford, Ire.
Nicholas Cooke	Boarder	Male	30	Knockany, Limerick, Ire.
William Barnes	Boarder	Male	31	Liverpool
Ann Smith	Servant	Female	24	Widnes
Catherine Smith	Servant	Female	18	Widnes
Alice Smith	Servant	Female	17	Widnes

18 St Patrick's Schools

... children delighted with the tadpoles ...
School Log Book, 12th May, 1915.

... found seven Std 11 children chasing a but-
terfly in Park Road at 9.20; took them into
school and marked them present ...
School Log Book, 4th June, 1915.

SINCE 1835, St Patrick's has been served by schools
in at least seven locations surrounding the church:
South Chester Street; Jenner Street; Upper Hill
Street; Park Place; Hyslop Street; Robertson Street and
Dexter Street. In 1844, there were 1,000 children of
school age; in 1921, 2,000; in 2020 a little over 200.

In 1832, the foundation stone of the first school was
laid in South Chester Street and the school was formally
opened in 1835. Within one building, the Boys' School
was on the first floor with the Girls' and Infants' School
on the ground floor. The Irish Christian Brothers took
charge of the boys in 1842 and continued until 1870,
when they left as a consequence of Forster's Education
Act. They founded the first evening continuation
schools in St Patrick's in 1842, attended by 120 students.

Financing the building of the first schools was partly
achieved by the preaching of an annual 'Charity
Sermon' in the setting of a formal High Mass, celebrated with a choir of professional musicians and
accompanied on the magnificent J. C. Bishop organ by
Samuel Webbe, St Patrick's celebrated organist. The
Liverpool Mercury gives details of some of these events:

St Patrick's Catholic Charity School

Friday 13th April, 1832

On Sunday next, the 15th instant, a charity sermon will be Preached by the Rev Francis Murphy, in St Patrick's Chapel, Park-place, in aid of the Funds for the Erection of the new school to be attached to that Chapel, the Foundation Stone of which was laid on St Patrick's Day (March 17) Inst.

Divine Service to commence at Eleven o'clock.

Considering the acknowledged utility of this Charity in bestowing the inestimable benefit of Education on the Children of the Poor, the Members of the Society count with confidence on the attendance and support of the benevolent and charitable of all persuasions. They acknowledge with gratitude the following liberal Donations:—

Legacy from the late Mr John Gerrard	£45 0 0
Mr Charles Chaloner	£20 0 0
Mr Edward Chaloner	£20 0 0
Mr Richard Shiel	£10 0 0
Mr Alexander Ryan	£10 0 0
Mr John Lynch	£10 0 0
Messrs Robert Roskell and Son	£10 0 0
Mr Patrick Leonard	£10 0 0
Rev Francis Murphy	£5 0 0
Mrs Corbally	£5 0 0
Messrs E. and J. Hore	£5 0 0
Mr Pelkington	£3 0 0
Mr Bunbury	£2 0 0
Mr G. Morris	£2 0 0
Rev Thos. Robinson	£1 0 0
Mr Corbally	£1 0 0

Miss Corbally	£1 0 0
Mr M'Laurin	£1 0 0
Mr M'Tear	£1 0 0
Mr Rattersby	£1 1 0
Mrs Howard	£1 0 0
Mr John Shepherd	£1 0 0
Mr D. Kennedy	£1 0 0
Mr Joseph Barrow	£1 0 0

Benevolent Society of St Patrick

Friday 14th March, 1834

The anniversary dinner will take place on St Patrick's Day, Monday next, the 17th March, at the Angel Hotel, Dale-street.

Richard Bryans, Esq. President

John Gordon, Esq. Vice-president

STEWARDS

Sir John Tobin	John Owens Johnson
Arthur Heywood	Matthew Nelson
Richard Shiel	John M'Cammon
William Latham	George Campbell
William Brown	John O'Neill
Edmund Hare	Morgan O'Connell
Nicholas Megraw	John Askew
Francis Jordan	Andrew Lendley

Dinner at the Table at Six o'clock

Tickets One Guinea each, apply to the Stewards, or at the Bar of the Angel Hotel.

The Supporters and Friends of the Charity are requested to attend the Annual Examination of the Scholars at the School, Pleasant-street, at Eleven o'clock in the morning.

St Patrick's Chapel

Friday 28th March, 1834

TO THE EDITOR OF THE LIVERPOOL MERCURY

Sir,—having read the notice in your last paper on the sermon, &c. at St Patrick's, to contribute towards a fund for the erection of a proper school to be annexed to that establishment, I observed that you omitted to mention the collection which was made on that occasion. I therefore take the liberty of begging you to insert the following remarks:— The chapel was extremely crowded, so that many in the galleries could not sit at all during the service, and numbers remained in the chapel yard who could not make their way into the building. After the service was over, the distinguished performers who had attracted this immense concourse, together with a few friends of Mr Murphy, (the head of the establishment,) adjourned to the Rev gentleman's house, where a handsome entertainment was prepared for them, and where the gratifying announcement was made, that a collection in the amount of £90 had been made at the chapel. The splendid organ, (unquestionably surpassing any other in the town, or in the country round about,) under the masterly management of Mr Webbe, rendered the service truly sublime on this occasion. This fine instrument has long languished from the want of a hand equal to its powers; and the congregation will be glad to hear that it is understood that this desideratum is hereafter to be supplied.

Yours, &c.

A member of St Patrick's and an enthusiastic lover of sacred music

St Patrick's Chapel—Charity Sermons

Friday 3rd November 1837

On Sunday, November 5, Solemn High Mass will be celebrated in the above Chapel. Two Sermons will be preached in aid of the Funds of St Patrick's Charity School; in the forenoon, at Eleven o'clock, by the Very Rev Dr Ullathorne, Vicar-general of New South Wales; and in the Afternoon, at half past Six o'clock, by the Rev Francis Murphy. Collections will be made after each sermon. The Choir will be augmented for the occasion, under the superintendence of Mr Webbe, who will preside at the organ.

St Patrick's Chapel—

Friday 31st August 1838

The annual sermons in behalf of the charity schools attached to this chapel will be preached on Sunday next, the 2nd of September. High mass will be performed, and there will be a grand selection of sacred music from the most celebrated compositions of Haydn and Mozart, including Zingarelli's magnificent Laudate, and Avison's 'Sound the loud Timbrel.' The principal vocalists will be Miss Whitnall, Miss Grant, and Mr G Horncastle, Of the Theatre-royal, aided by an efficient choir, Mr Webbe presiding at the organ. We understand that the schools afford the blessings of education and virtuous training to between three and four hundred poor children, and also that they are admirably conducted. For further particulars we refer to the advertisement, which will be found in another column.

In 1844, an order of nuns, known as the Faithful Companions of Jesus ('the Sisters'), came to Liverpool and opened a boarding school in Great George's Square;

they also agreed to Fr William Parker's request to take charge of the Girls' and Infants' Schools at St Patrick's.

It was considered necessary for Catholic children to have their own schools since the Tory majority on Liverpool's Town Council maintained an education policy between 1841 and 1892 which insisted that every child attending a council school must use the Authorised Version of the Bible and a common form of prayer—a policy which the Catholic clergy could not accept. As a result, parishes like St Patrick's built their own schools.

The Sisters also took a very broad view of education, following the example of the Christian Brothers. When the day school finished, women came for instruction and preparation for the Sacraments, perhaps 200 per night. In 1844, Fr Parker wrote to their superior, 'In our many heavy parish duties, it is a relief for us to be able to hand over these poor women to your Sisters'.[30] Mother Xavier O'Neill was the first head of the school. In 1845, there were between 500 and 600 children enrolled; in the evenings, she taught the adults. On Sunday mornings, she accompanied the children to Mass; in the evenings she instructed the adults again. She died of Typhus Fever on 30th April, 1846 as did Fr Parker on 27th April, 1847. Mother Julia Slack was Head 1870–1886. She was the only certified teacher in the school; her staff consisted entirely of pupil-teachers and monitoresses.

The Liverpool Mercury gives a more detailed picture of the realities of providing education for St Patrick's children at this time, in its issues of 20th January, 1843 and 14th July, 1848:

---

[30] M. C. McCarren et al, *With Devotedness and Love 1844-1994* (FCJ, 1994), p. 16.

New Catholic School

Friday 20th January, 1843

A meeting of Roman Catholics was held last night in the large room, Blundell-street (lately occupied as a penny theatre,) preliminary to its being opened as a school for the education of the poor children who have been turned out of the Corporation schools. The room has been cleaned and refitted, and will be capable of holding about two hundred children. The meeting was well attended by the inhabitants of the neighbourhood. The Rev William Parker, one of the ministers of St Patrick's Chapel, opened the business, and, in the course of a very excellent and temperate address, referred to the conduct of the present Town Council in excluding the children of Catholic parents from the Corporation Schools, by the introduction of religious tests. He remarked on the injustice and inhumanity of such proceedings, yet he could not help feeling that good would come out of evil. He, with his colleagues, in collecting subscriptions for the new schools, had met with the most friendly feeling and the most generous assurances, as well as pecuniary aid from many Protestants, and he might mention, for he believed he was at liberty to do so, that John Ripley, Esq. of 23 Canning-street, had presented £20 towards the object they had in view. Last year, at this time, there were only 500 scholars in the schools of St Patrick, but now there were 820, and they expected, when the school in Blundell-street was opened, that they would have about 1000 children under their care at that end of the town. Mr Parker then informed the meeting that, on and after Sunday week, mass would be said in that room every Sunday, and there would be preaching morning and evening. On Sundays it would be St Patrick's chapel, and on week days a school attached to St Patrick's church.

Referring to the spiritual destitution of the neighbourhood he said that in the next street, Crosbie-street, and he had the names of all the persons down, there were 1200, excepting four, Catholics alone. These were sufficient to support a priest themselves, and he, therefore, called upon those present to subscribe their pennies, and do what they could towards the expenses of their new place. They had taken the room for 8 years, and he hoped before the expiration of that period, that they would have a new place of worship built in that neighbourhood. The Rev Mr McCormick, of Londonderry, who is to officiate at the room on Sundays, made a few observations to the meeting, which were well received. The Rev Mr Frith, of St Patrick's, in the course of a few appropriate observations, said there was nothing which so much tended to elevate the Catholics, or any other body of persons, as giving them a good religious and moral education. He concluded by proposing the following resolution:—"That the Liberal Protestants who have come forward so honourably and so generously to assist the Catholic body in general are deserving of our warmest thanks." The Rev William Grayston, in a few able remarks, seconded the resolution, which was carried by acclamation. After a few concluding observations from the Rev W. Parker, the meeting separated. A collection was made at the doors towards defraying the expenses of altering the room.

School Examination

Friday 14th July, 1848

Tuesday last being the day fixed for the examination of the boys of St Patrick's Schools, there was present a large and respectable attendance of the Catholics of the district, amongst whom were Revs J. J. Crook, E. Kenrick, B. O'Reilly,

Mr Reardon, the superior general of the Christian Brothers, Mr A. Ryan, Mr J. Houlgrave, Mr W. Banbury, Captain Choldish, Mrs Charles Moore, Miss Ryan, &c. &c.

There are upwards of 950 poor children receiving education in the schools, of which 500 are boys, and the remainder girls. The course of education taught in the boys' school comprises reading, writing, arithmetic, grammar, geography, mathematics, and the use of the globes. On each of these branches they were examined at some length, and acquitted themselves most respectably. Boys only twelve years old passed very difficult sentences in the English grammar, and not a few manifested a knowledge of mathematics and the use of the globes that would reflect credit on schools of higher pretentions. The thoughtfulness of their responses was evident to the most superficial observer, and afforded a pleasing contrast to that hurried and unseeming manner which seldom accompanies an exercise of the mind. These schools are conducted by the Christian Brothers, and the neat and cleanly appearance of their pupils, together with the numbers that are weekly applying for admission, attest the advantages that are derived from their excellent presidency. Were it not for the labours of these humble philanthropists, whose unobtrusive lives are unreservedly dedicated to the instruction of poor children, hundreds of the families of our Catholic townsmen would be deprived of the blessings of education. They are most sensibly impressed with the truth that "of all the men we meet with, nine out of ten are what they are, good or evil, useful or not, by their education; it is that which makes the greatest difference in mankind. The little or almost insensible impressions on our tender infancy have very important and lasting consequences—that virtue is the hard and valuable part to be aimed at in education; and that all other considerations and accomplishments should give way and be postponed to this." To many liberal Protestants it is due to acknowledge the kind support they have given to these schools, who have thereby afforded an evidence of that instructive charity which elevates itself above the mindless distinctions of sects or creeds.—M. A. McD.

In common with other Liverpool schools, St Patrick's responded to important political or national events. For instance, to celebrate the ending of the Crimean War in 1856, the schoolchildren formed a parade through Liverpool's streets. St Patrick's led the Catholic contingent, following their parish priest, Fr Kenrick. Other Log Book entries include:

15th June, 1897: Holiday for the remainder of this week in honour of the Diamond Jubilee of her Majesty, Queen Victoria.

22nd June, 1911: Distribution of Halfpennies for Coronation Day.

25th September, 1916: Private Proctor VC came to show his Cross to the children.

As the numbers of children continued to grow, new school accommodation was needed. Canon Goethals opened the new schools in Hyslop Street on 2nd April, 1872. The girls and infants moved there, forming two separate schools in one building. Nevertheless, demand continued to outstrip supply. The School Log Book entry for 10th March, 1877 reads,

School overcrowded, about 200 children belonging to neighbouring districts dismissed by the manager (Canon Goethals) on account of the overcrowded state of the school. Great confusion caused by the dismissal of the children. Parents entreating for their re-admission.

Part of the solution was to develop new provision in the new parish of Mount Carmel which emerged from St Patrick's in 1878; and additional classrooms were built in South Chester Street, with alterations to the old building in 1888, at a cost of £1,667. The process continued with the foundation stone of a new Infants' School in Robertson Street being laid on 22nd September, 1894 by Mgr James Carr, the Diocesan Inspector of Schools. This school opened on 27th May, 1895; the eventual total cost was £3484. Canon Goethals annotated his own copy of *Gleanings* with the words, 'Taken over by St Malachy's 1900'.

Mother Hilda Fletcher became head of Hyslop Street in 1886 and retired in 1928, after 42 years in the same post, at the age of 64. On her retirement, the Director of Education wrote, 'Your influence … has been at once an inspiration and a source of strength'. As the population of Liverpool continued to grow, the development of new school buildings was essential.

In addition to overcrowding, poverty was another problem confronting the schools. The Log Book records that, on Christmas Day, 1895, the Sisters served breakfast 'for 240 of the poorest children whose hungry looking eyes brightened at the sight of a plentiful supply of food'. Moreover, the Sisters 'had the satisfaction of seeing them part with clothing which hardly deserved the name, being but a collection of rags'.

Mother Hilda was keen to prepare her girls for employment when they left school and to develop their home making skills. Thus, in 1899, she was able to persuade the Liverpool School Board that dressmaking, cookery and laundry work should be incorporated into the ordinary curriculum; by 1918, this had been extended to include housecraft, first aid, home nursing and care of babies. In addition, Mother Hilda developed the evening classes to include dressmaking and introduced a lending library. A school inspector's report of this period states 'Reading has been taught in such a way that the older girls have been led to appreciate books'.

Mother Hilda also worked hard to instil in her children pride in themselves and their local area. This can be seen in the bowers of foliage erected in the streets to celebrate Canon Goethals' Golden Jubilee in 1913 and in the May processions, with the girls dressed in pure white, wearing silver wreaths, and carrying twigs of lime as they walked through the streets.

Pride in achievement could also be developed through music in both secular songs and liturgical chant. A feature of St Patrick's musical life was the singing of Gregorian Plain Chant; Dom Anselm Burge, OSB, composed a new setting of '*Quid Retribuam Domino*' for Canon Goethals' Golden Jubilee Mass in 1913. In addition, the children were encouraged to look outside their local area. In 1923, for instance, 1,500 had a tea party in Calderstones Park.

Perhaps Mother Hilda's achievement is best summarised in the Inspector's Report of 1905: 'A delightful school. Everything that is done is done well'. Mother Hilda died in October, 1934. The *Bellerive Annals* describe the funeral:

> ... a vast congregation which not only filled the church but assisted in reverent silence outside in the pouring rain ... music supplied by the senior children of the school ... the streets were lined as for a royal cortege.

By this time, the new school in Jenner Street had been opened on 1st May, 1927 and the Canon Goethals Memorial School had been opened on 15th October, 1928, with Mother Margaret Mary as its first Head. She had to cope with all the difficulties of the Second World War years—evacuation, devastation, loss of faith. In 1953, she moved across the road to head the Girls' School where soon the children had distinctive uniforms: light green blouses, with dark green skirts, tie and cardigan. She worked very closely in partnership with the parish priest, Mgr Curry.

In 1959 Mother Margaret Mary was succeeded by Sister Helen Downes who eventually became Head of St Martin's, the new Secondary Modern School for Girls which opened in April, 1969. She was succeeded by Sister Mary Jordan 1969–1976. St Martin's Secondary Modern School for Boys had opened in May, 1962 with Mr R. J. Harrison as Head. Like St Martin's Girls', it catered for senior children from the parishes of St Patrick's, St Vincent's and St Peter's. By 1984, both of these schools had disappeared, being absorbed in the Archdiocesan reorganisation of its Liverpool secondary schools; this also was the year when the Faithful Companions of Jesus finally withdrew from St Patrick's schools.

In more recent years, the parish has been served by a single school, St Patrick's Primary, in South Chester Street, just behind the church. Reflecting local population trends, statistics in the Liverpool Archdiocesan Directory reveal that the number of children attending the school declined from 351 in 1993 to 134 in 2010, since when the numbers have increased reaching 205 in 2015.

The role of the school in 2020/2021 is described by its current head, Mrs Joanne Lewis:

I have the honour of being the headteacher of this truly wonderful school. We are proud of (and endlessly fascinated by) the long history of St Patrick's Primary School and the service it has provided for many years to its pupils and the wider community. In 2020, our desire is as strong as ever to care for and nurture our pupils through this crucial stage of their education and to prepare them for life in the modern world. Our role in supporting the parish and the local area continues to strengthen and evolve, as we seek to enable our pupils to become responsible global citizens in the twenty first century. For our families, too, we strive not just to educate their children, but to be an oasis in the community for those who need support and sanctuary.

Sanctuary is the key word here. The school is based in a culturally diverse area with a strong sense of community, but one that faces socio-economic challenges. St Patrick's received a School of Sanctuary Award in 2018, meaning that we have shown our commitment to being a safe and welcoming place for those seeking sanctuary. This has included people whose lives were in danger in their own country, who have troubles at home or are just looking for a space of safety. As a School of Sanctuary, our ambition is to help our students, staff and wider community to understand what it means to be seeking sanctuary and to extend a welcome to everyone as equal, valued members of the school community. St Patrick's is a school that is proud to be a place of safety and inclusion for all.

Inevitably, the cultural make-up of St Patrick's Primary School has changed a lot since it first opened in 1835. We are a Catholic school, but we welcome a significant number of children from non-Christian backgrounds (mainly thanks to a vibrant Muslim population in the area) and many children speak English as a second language. However, at the heart of everything we think and do at St Patrick's remain the Christian principles of peace, love and understanding. We believe that following these principles will help us to show mutual care, respect and forgiveness. Indeed, our relationship with St Patrick's Church is one which we value as much as ever, providing many benefits to our school, not just in terms of nurturing the children's religious education and guiding their own personal journeys of faith, but also serving as a welcoming setting for numerous whole-school, multi-faith celebrations.

It is difficult to summarise the role the school plays in the community, but we certainly believe that, by promoting good relationships between home, school, parish and community, we are doing so to the benefit of all. It is not a one-way street; whether it is by raising money on charity drives, organising food bank collections or carol singing in local care homes, our pupils gain a great deal from their experiences, and that really brings us back to our ultimate focus: the children.

Our motto is 'Be the best you can be'. We have a dedicated team of staff who are committed to providing excellent education and wider opportunities for the children in their care. We offer an extremely rich and broad curriculum, ensuring that the children have the opportunity to enjoy their time in school, and to develop a love of learning. We work together as a school, as a parish, as a community to help each individual towards happiness, self-belief, independence and fulfilment.

That is St Patrick's Primary School in 2020 and I am extremely proud to be a part of it.

19 A VISIT TO ST PATRICK'S CHURCH

Exterior

ISITORS LOOKING AT the west front of the church will particularly wish to see the following four features:

* The free standing Celtic cross (1898), commemorating the ten Liverpool priests who died during the 1847 Typhus epidemic and of whom the *Liverpool Mercury* said on 19th June, 1847 'They laid down their lives for their flocks ... (in the) ... conscientious discharge of ... their duty...'

* The rectangular stone plaque on the west wall recording that the ground floor of St Patrick's Chapel is free in perpetuity for the use of all worshippers.

* The large stone statue of St Patrick was originally designed to stand outside the offices of the St Patrick Assurance Company of Ireland Ltd., in Dublin. This company was established on 11th May, 1824; it rapidly got into difficulties in 1826; by 1829 it had ceased trading. As the company offered Marine Insurance facilities in Liverpool, it would have been known to James Brancker, a large scale importer of sugar. When its assets were sold off, Brancker took the opportunity to acquire the statue, and presented it to St Patrick's Church, to stand on a plinth on the West wall of the church, above an inscription reading, with a Latin date, 'The gift of James Brancker 1827'. No evidence has been found

for the assertion in Burke's 'Catholic History of Liverpool' (1910) that Brancker ordered the statue from a Dublin firm of sculptors, though it is possible that the sculptors may have been happy to sell the statue to Brancker if the bankrupt insurance company which had ordered it could no longer afford to pay for it. His reasons for making this gift are explored more fully in the chapter on James Brancker and his associates.

• The metal door, leading to the crypt containing burial vaults and pits. Amongst others, Fr William Parker, Rector of St Patrick's, who died of Typhus, is buried here. The adjacent vault, entered through an iron door bearing the date '1828', contains the coffins of Peter Roberts and four of his family, with a further coffin buried in the undercroft of the vault.

Behind the east wall, adjacent to South Chester Street, is the site of the former vestries, demolished when the area below the west gallery was partitioned off and partly developed as a new vestry. The lavabo there, from the old vestry, is a tribute to Canon Goethals. The church is surrounded by its former graveyard. In the corner, overlooking Park Place, is the Memorial set up by the Burns family recording their five children who died aged between seven years and five months. The Burial Books of St Patrick's record that, between 1827 and 1841, at least 7,466 individuals were buried either in the graveyard or the crypt, many of them children.

The bell and its belfry are a later addition to the church. Originally cast by James Sheridan of Dublin in 1844, the bell was remade by Taylors Bellfounders of Loughborough in 1951.

Interior

The interior is much larger than it seems at first sight; this is because the area below the west gallery has been partitioned off to provide a meeting room and other services.

The east end of the church is dominated by an enormous painting depicting the crucifixion of Jesus Christ. Entitled 'Le Calvaire', it was painted by M Nicaise de Keyser, who was born in Antwerp in 1813 and completed the painting in 1834, when he was 21 years old. At the Antwerp Salon of that year, 'Le Calvaire' won the award of 'Picture of the Year'. The painting was commissioned for a Catholic church in Manchester. The church authorities were so delighted with it that they gave de Keyser a gratuity of £100. Unfortunately, the church collapsed before the painting could be hung there. After exhibition in several English cities, it found a home at St Patrick's in 1835; originally 30ft wide and 22ft high, it had to be modified to fit in the available space. The 'Liverpool Daily Post' of 19th January, 1901 describes it as 'One of the finest altar pieces in the United Kingdom'.

Balancing 'Le Calvaire', the rear of the church is dominated by the west gallery, surmounted by a magnificent classical organ case. The gallery has a seating capacity of 600 and is a physical symbol of the influence of those who paid bench rents for accommodation there in 1827.

The Organ

The organ at St Patrick's was built by James Chapman Bishop (1783–1854) of Marylebone, one of the leading organ builders of the first half of the nineteenth century. He started his business in March 1807 and eventually established a close connection with the Catholic Church in England, which had begun a rapid expansion of church building after the passing of the Catholic Relief Act of 1791 and the Catholic Emancipation Act of 1829. Each of these new 'chapels' required a pipe organ, and Bishop's entry into this field may be dated to 1830 when he built the first two of over 150 instruments for Catholic churches, one for Brighton and the other for St Patrick's in Liverpool. The influential organist whose family founded the music publishing company, Vincent Novello, was an admirer of Bishop's work and his recommendations resulted in Bishop being commissioned to build organs for a number of Catholic churches in London. Bishop did some work on the organ at the Royal Sardinian Embassy Chapel in London in 1827 where Novello's friends, Samuel Webbe Senior and Junior were organists. The Webbes worked hard to maintain the highest standards of Catholic music, particularly at the Embassy Chapels. Laurence Elvin states that Novello 'by reason of his technique and knowledge of organ building, was constantly asked to demonstrate new organs, as well as to design and supervise their construction, hence his acquaintance with Bishop'.[31]

The reasons for the choice of Bishop, a London-based organ builder, to build the organ at St Patrick's in Liverpool are not fully known but, given that Samuel Webbe the Younger (c 1770–1843) became the first organist at St Patrick's, the explanation may well lie here. Webbe had succeeded his father at the Royal Sardinian Embassy. With his father, he produced a considerable quantity of Catholic church music,

---

[31] L. Elvin, *Bishop and Son, Organ Builders* (Elvin, 1984), p. 188.

including 'A Collection of Motets and Antiphons' (1792). He then settled in Liverpool as organist to the Unitarian Chapel in Paradise Street in 1798. About 1817, he returned to London, as organist of the Spanish Embassy Chapel, and from there returned to Liverpool as organist at St Patrick's, where, in conjunction with Novello, he may well have been able to design his own instrument, to be built by Bishop.

Further contemporary evidence of the origins of the organ may be found in Bishop's own records: 'To a new Organ with three rows of keys. Compafs (sic) from GG with GG #. Opened in July (1830).' The Liverpool Mercury has two references to the organ: the issue for 11th June, 1830 notes that the organ 'had arrived on Saturday last, and is now in progress of erection'. The issue for 23rd July 1830 is more detailed: 'St Patrick's Chapel—On Wednesday last, the new organ at this chapel was opened, and, after an excellent sermon by the Rev Mr McDonnel, a collection of £35 was made towards defraying the expenses. We are told by one whom we consider a competent judge that the organ is one of the finest, IF NOT THE FINEST, in the town.' The pedigree of this instrument could hardly be more impressive and Webbe's interest becomes obvious.

The organ was cleaned and repaired by Gray and Davison in 1888. Thornsby's 'Dictionary of Organs and Organists' (1912) states that the organ was restored by T. C. Lewis, but gives no date; this firm certainly undertook its tuning and maintenance between 1896 and 1910. This work may have been influenced by W. J. Bowden, who became organist at St Patrick's in 1887, at the age of 30, and continued until 1931. He would also have supervised the work when, in 1910, the organ was rebuilt by Rushworth and Dreaper at a cost of

£300, of which £150 was donated by Mr Carnegie. In 1953, Rushworth and Dreaper repaired wartime damage and again rebuilt the organ. In 1988, it was comprehensively examined by Mr Mark Venning of Harrison and Harrison, organ builders of Durham, who suggested that it had begun life as a two manual organ, with a Tenor C Swell and a simple stop of pedal pipes. It was progressively enlarged in the nineteenth century, but much early work remains. The central portion of the handsome organ case has been modified to accommodate larger Open Diapason pipes, with the original pipes re-located inside the case.

Organ Specification 2020

This is a three manual and pedal pipe organ, manuals c to g3, 56 notes and pedals c to f1, 30 notes. Attached, drawstop console, tubular pneumatic action.

Swell	Great	Choir	Pedal
Tremulant			
Horn 8ft	Clarion 4ft	Clarinet 8ft	Bass Flute 8ft
Oboe 8ft	Trumpet 8ft	Octave 4ft	Bourdon 16ft
Piccolo 2ft	Mixture III	Flute 4ft	Open Diapason 16ft
Principal 4ft	Fifteenth 2ft	Dulciana 8ft	
Stop Diapason 8ft	Twelfth 2 2/3 ft	Clarabella 8ft	
Salicional 8ft	Principal 4ft		
Open Diapason 8ft	Stopped Diapason 8ft		
	Open Diapason ii 8ft		
	Open Diapason i 8ft		

Couplers: Swell to Great; Swell to Pedal; Great to Pedal; Choir to Pedal; Swell to Choir; Swell Octave; Swell Sub-octave.

Accessories: Balanced Swell Pedal; 2 composition pedals to Swell; 3 composition pedals to Great and Pedal. Electric blower.

When, in 2020, a major grant was received to enable repairs to be made to the West wall, it became necessary to dismantle that part of the Pedal Organ which was bolted to the inside of the wall, to provide necessary access for the builders. This provided an opportunity to repair parts of the rear of the organ which had been inaccessible since 1953, and to clean the interior of the instrument.

The best view of the interior of the church is from the organist's bench in the gallery. From this vantage point, it can be seen how the sanctuary has lost much of its magnificence, although it is still flanked by neo-classical statues of St Matthew and St Mark in niches, high up to the left and right. The accompanying photographs show how the original High Altar was significantly elevated, approached by a flight of seven curving steps and enclosed within a semi-circular communion rail. The original High Altar was replaced in 1867, at a cost of £500, to the designs of the architect J. F. Bentley who also built Westminster Cathedral and the High Altar at Bishop Eton Church, Liverpool. In keeping with the architectural and liturgical fashions of the time, the altar at St Patrick's featured a tall, tapering Benediction Throne, with angels to each side, honouring the Real Presence. The sanctuary steps were covered with parquetry (white oak, inlaid with walnut) in 1905, at a cost of £125. With the new electric lighting, installed in 1903, the entire sanctuary ensemble must have been striking.

The 1978 Anniversary Souvenir shows how, by that date, the High Altar had been simplified by the removal of the Benediction Throne and the rectangular Tabernacle below it, and their replacement by a domed, brass Tabernacle.[32] A new marble 'reredos' with a curved top was decorated with two Celtic motifs in mosaic. The altar rails were still in place.

Inevitably, the combination of the painting, framed by the giant Corinthian columns, the gilded ceiling bosses and the chandeliers, lead the eye to the 2020 sanctuary, now only a shadow of its former self. This brutal re-ordering, imposed after the Second Vatican Council, has swept the reredos away, together with the altar rails, leaving a fragment of Bentley's work as a free standing altar, with a wooden table supporting the domed Tabernacle occupying the space previously filled by the High Altar. The rectangular (Bentley?) Tabernacle has been re-located in the South East corner of the church. Hopefully, it will be possible to soften these changes to give the church some hint of what the original architects intended, and thus more integrity, while still accommodating the requirements of contemporary liturgy.

In the north east corner is an arched marble relief of the Holy Family, probably from the 1891 St Joseph's Altar by Boulton of Cheltenham.

Visitors should also see the fourteen Stations of the Cross, a tribute to Canon Kenrick who died in 1860; the statue of St Patrick and the Pieta in the church porch; the painted Paschal candlestick; and the jewelled Benediction monstrance. Of particular interest is a large, gilded chalice presented to the church by Bishop Robert Brindle DSO, 1837–1916, in memory of his parents. Brindle was born in Liverpool and

---

[32]   A. J. Hocter, *St Patrick's 150th Anniversary Souvenir* (Liverpool 1978).

ordained priest in 1862. His bravery as an army chaplain in Egypt caused him to be widely regarded as a military hero and he was recommended for a knighthood. He was Bishop of Nottingham 1901–1916 and was buried with full military honours. Before Princess Victoria Ena of Battenberg, the niece of King Edward VII, could marry King Alfonso XIII of Spain in 1906, Spanish custom dictated that she should become a Catholic. King Edward considered that Brindle would be a person of sufficient standing, acceptable to all parties, who could provide her with the necessary religious instruction. As a token of thanks for his work, the princess presented Brindle with a set of church altar plate of which this chalice formed part.

20 JAMES BRANCKER AND FAMILY, DANIEL O'CONNELL AND ST PATRICK'S CHURCH

HE PERIOD 1810–1840 was largely one of good relationships between Liverpool Town Council and members of the local Roman Catholic community, who were regarded with almost benevolent toleration. Thus, the Mayor and Aldermen attended the High Mass for the opening of the Church of St Nicholas, Hawke Street, in 1815 for which they had presented the land on which it was built.

James Brancker (1790–1852) was a prosperous Liverpool businessman who, with his brother, Sir Thomas (1783–1853), a former mayor, operated a large sugar refinery in Matthew Street, in the centre of the town. Liverpool Record Office preserves a wide ranging collection of papers relating to the Brancker family. The documents show that the family was descended from John Brancker, who lived about 1430. His direct descendant was Thomas Brancker, Headmaster of Barnstaple High School in 1630. By 1676, the Brancker family had moved to Liverpool, becoming involved in the gold and silver industry, overseas trading and sugar refining. They made a very significant contribution to the development of Liverpool as a centre of world trade and manufacturing, where they were active in political, business and cultural affairs throughout the Nineteenth Century and beyond. For example, John Barnes Brancker laid the foundation stone of the Liverpool Philharmonic Hall in 1846;

Henry Brancker, a friend of Ernest Shackleton, was involved with the British Legation in the Argentine Republic; and John Brancker was Chairman of the Mersey Docks and Harbour Board, 1890–1899. As the family grew, its members became involved in many aspects of British life at national level also. Thus, the Rev Thomas Brancker was a chaplain to the forces in 1917; Air Vice Marshal Sir William Sefton Brancker KCB was killed when Airship R101 crashed in France in October, 1930; and Flying Officer Henry Paul Brancker was killed in action in 1942. Dr Winifred Mary Brancker, CBE, 1914–2010, his sister, was the first woman to become president of the British Veterinary Association (1967) and celebrated her 90th birthday by taking a flying lesson. The Brancker family continues to be represented on Merseyside in the person of Michael Brancker, a tree surgeon based in Ormskirk, who was born in 1952 in the West Indies, the home of cricketer Rawle Cecil Brancker.

James Brancker was married twice, firstly to Jane Moss, in 1815 and, after her death in 1841, to Ann Symonds, in 1842. Jane appears to have been an invalid throughout her married life, probably as a consequence of obstetrical complications. When not in Liverpool, James lived with her at their country house, Croft Lodge, Ambleside, which he rebuilt in 1830 and sold in 1841, after Jane's death. With Ann Symonds, he had three children, Annie Jane (1843–1917); James (1845–1864); and Mary (1846–1940). The Brancker Collection in Liverpool Record Office contains a letter, written on 22nd February, 1852, just after James Brancker's death, by his ward, Jane Dorothea Claude to her friend, Mary Louisa Cannan containing a character sketch of her Guardian: 'He was very generous and kind to those he employed and always attracted people to him. At Ambleside, the people quite worshipped him and thought as much of his little boy as they would have done of the Prince of Wales, I believe … Never had a man a kinder, more generous friend …'

Brancker was a High Tory and a member of the Church of England. His marriage to Jane Moss had taken place at the Parish Church of St Thomas, Park Lane, Liverpool, where his daughter, Annie Jane, was baptised on 20th September, 1843. It may seem odd, therefore, that he should present a large statue of its patron saint to the new Catholic Church of St Patrick in 1827, to be put up in a prominent position on its front wall, directly overlooking the road. The explanation may lie in the fact that, like many of his Liverpool merchant colleagues, he was an ardent supporter of Daniel O'Connell (1775–1847) and his movement for Catholic Emancipation, which resulted in the Emancipation Act of 1829, admitting English and Irish Roman Catholics to Parliament.

Educated partly in France, Daniel O'Connell became a very successful lawyer and political agitator, the leader of the movement for Catholic Emancipation. He adopted the liberal ideas of the Age of the Enlightenment, being greatly influenced by Thomas Paine's 'The Rights of Man' and the ideas of Jeremy Bentham. Writing in 'The Irish Times' on 22nd December, 2020, Olivia O'Leary says of him, 'When vast English and American fortunes were being made out of the Slave Trade, he became one of the world's most outspoken campaigners to abolish slavery.' In January 1836, O'Connell made his first public appearance in Liverpool—at the Corn Exchange, Brunswick Street. Interestingly, his ideas attracted wide support among the

Liverpool merchant classes, including Brancker. Evidence for this may be found in a report in the *Liverpool Mercury* of 6th June, 1836 detailing how Brancker took the chair at a public meeting to raise money for O'Connell's campaigns.

Thus, when placed in a prominent position, high up on the front wall of St Patrick's Church, the statue was not only a very appropriate symbol outside a Catholic church, but can also be considered as a silent, subtle public statement of local support for O'Connell and his cause as the campaign for Catholic Emancipation reached its culmination in 1829.

The following reference to the statue appeared in the *Liverpool Mercury*.

> Society of St Patrick
>
> Vote of thanks to James Brancker, Esq
>
> At a meeting of the Society of St Patrick, held in the Large Room, Mersey-street, on Sunday, the 14th instant, the Meeting was favoured with a communication from Mr Brancker, (through the medium of Dr Collins,) intimating that gentleman's intention of presenting a valuable and highly-finished STATUE OF ST PATRICK to the Society: on which occasion the following Resolution was proposed, and unanimously adopted: –
>
> *Resolved,*—That the sincere and grateful thanks of the Society of St Patrick be presented to James Brancker Esq. for his munificent gift; and that so splendid a proof of Protestant liberality be gratefully acknowledged in the Liverpool papers, and also inserted on the records of the Institution, to convey to future generations the high respect which the Society entertain for the giver of so expensive and suitable an ornament.
>
> *(Signed)* Richard Kehoe, President.

Mersey-street, Liverpool, Oct. 14, 1827

The STATUE OF ST PATRICK has arrived from Dublin, and was delivered to the Society, free of all charges, yesterday, the 1st of November, and is considered, by competent judges, to be one of the most correct and best finished pieces of Statuary in the United Kingdom.

A further insight into Brancker and his business may be found in a report of a major fire at his refinery, in the *Liverpool Mercury* of 29th December 1843, reproduced here as an appendix.

21 THE BUILDING, ITS REPAIR AND RESTORATION

WRITING IN JUNE 2021, Liverpool Archdiocesan Surveyor Kirk Williams, who has responsibility for maintaining the church structure, has provided the following perspective.

Built between 1821–27, St Patrick's is Liverpool's earliest surviving Catholic church still in use as a place of worship. It was the first Catholic church to be built in the south end of the city and today is prominent landmark on an elevated site overlooking one of the main thoroughfares from the city centre. It is a Grade II* Listed building and considered one of the most historic and architecturally significant churches in Liverpool.

The architect was John Slater. He was a joiner based in Seel Street, Liverpool, who also practised as an architect. In 1812 he presented a design for an altar-piece for a Catholic chapel in the Liverpool Academy's exhibition. Between 1812 and 1816 he was also employed by Thomas Scarisbrick to carry out extensive alterations to Scarisbrick Hall, Lancashire. The alterations were carried out in a Gothic style and Slater was assisted by Thomas Rickman with the designs.

Slater's design was one of several plans submitted to the Society of St Patrick. As already noted, within the Society's first report dated December 2nd, 1816, it states that they had selected one proposal "combining elegance of appearance, economy of expense and convenience of the structure, with dimensions of a very large extent."

The plans calculated that the building would accommodate 1200 persons on the ground floor, free of all expense, and in the gallery containing 106 benches, accommodation for a further 600 persons. The cost of constructing the church including the land purchase was estimated at £9,000. To reach this figure the Society of St Patrick was entirely dependent upon charitable contributions, except in so far as they would also be assisted by the sale of seats in the gallery. If all the seats were sold it would produce £2,876 and bring in an annual revenue of £370. The poor may also have contributed what they could by way of weekly subscriptions.

Illustration 9 shows plans of the gallery at the altar end, an elevation of the altar and a section through the galleries. They are unsigned and undated but are thought to show the original arrangement and are possibly drawn by Slater himself.

Between August and October 1818, the Society purchased the existing site from the Earl of Sefton, having previously considered land on Great Georges Place and Upper Parliament Street.

The Foundation Stone was laid on the 17th March 1821 and celebrated with a major ceremony and procession. An account of this event is described earlier in this book.

The church is a solid brick structure with sandstone dressings that have been overpainted. The exterior is quite plain in its design. The reason for this is no doubt due to the need for economy of construction and the fact that it was not until the Relief Act of 1829 that Catholics were able to build churches with steeples. The Relief Acts of 1778 and 1791 had legalized the building of Catholic churches with the stipulation that they were to be of simple construction and "without bell or tower".

What is interesting about the design of the exterior are the two porches and their porticoes. These porches look like transepts and have the effect of turning what could be considered a Greek rectangular church into a cruciform plan. The long arm of this Latin cross constitutes the nave of the church, whilst the short arms house the ground floor entrances and elegant timber staircases that lead up to the galleries. Each porch has a portico with four Greek Doric sandstone columns. These porticos would have originally had a roof structure which has sadly been lost over time.

The gabled west front of the church has a stone cross in the pediment and below this on a second storey pedestal there is a large statue of St Patrick, which was erected in November 1827, as a gift by James Brancker. It is reputed that this statue was the first Catholic emblem to be erected in Liverpool since the Reformation. At the time it was considered by some to be one of the most correct and best finished pieces of Statuary in the United Kingdom. Further detail on the statue's donor James Brancker can be found in the chapter on his family.

The scaffolding from the recent restoration work to the west gable allowed us to take a closer look at the statue of St Patrick. We knew some things about its condition, most notably the damage to the right hand. Legend has it that an anti-Catholic mob attacked the church on St Patrick's Day 1848. A curate at the time, Rev Bernard O'Reilly, later Bishop O'Reilly, is said to have led his people into Park Place to defend the church and succeeded in repulsing the attack with the assistance of many special constables, sworn in for the purpose. Although the attack was thwarted, one group of the mob got a rope around the hand of the statue but failed to dislodge it, pulling off only the finger of the right hand. If you look up at the statue from Park Road you will see the finger is still missing.

The statue is made of stone and whilst it is unlikely to have been painted originally, it has been painted a number of times over the years. The multiple layers of paint were breaking down and peeling from the surface due to age and exposure. We took the opportunity to remove the paintwork carefully so that the stone beneath could be viewed and assessed. Illustrations 59 and 60 show the statue before and after the paint has been carefully removed. Note the fine detailing on the face, stole and mitre that had been hidden beneath the previous layers of paint.

The statue was also missing its staff. Thankfully, parish volunteer Tony McKean found the upper section of the staff in the north stairwell and kept it safe for a number of years in the hope that it could one day be reinstated. That time is now, and we have made a new lower section of the cross and fixed in back into position.

It is likely that further restoration of the statue will be required in the future and given its historic significance, any such work should only be done after appropriate advice has been obtained from an accredited conservation specialist.

Underneath the statue of St Patrick is a sandstone plaque with an inscription which reads:

SAINT PATRICK'S CHAPEL BUILT BY PUBLIC SUBSCRIPTION

Under the express stipulation that the whole of the ground floor should for ever remain free for the accommodation of all.

> Keep therefore the words of this Covenant and
> fulfil them Deut. XXIX 9.
>
> Begun A.D. 1821
>
> Finished AD

You will notice that the date of finishing remains blank and has never been entered. This is to signify that the work of St Patrick's has never been finished and will continue into the future.

The presence of this plaque underlines the importance of its message to those responsible for founding and maintaining the church. It is also clearly stipulated in the historical documentation that still exists for the church.

The continuing work of the church is symbolised by the Celtic Cross in front of the west front of the church and of great historic significance since it stands as a memorial to ten Catholic Priests of Liverpool, who lost their lives while attending to the sick during the typhus epidemic that struck the city in 1847. The memorial was erected in 1898, commemorating the 50th anniversary of their heroism.

The bell tower is thought to have been added around 1844. That is the year that the original bell was cast by the James Sheridan Foundry, Dublin. Illustration 15 was taken circa 1900 and shows how the bell tower may have looked originally. The bell tower is located on the north transept; it is square in plan with arched headed louvred openings on all elevations and there is a Fleuree Cross in a central position on the lead covered roof. Over recent decades the tower had been boarded over with plywood sheets. This resulted in the original arched heads and louvres being hidden from view. The recent restoration works have allowed us to address several problems with the bell tower. The plywood over boarding had become rotten as had areas of the tower's framework. Some of the louvres had been crudely cut back to allow for the installation of the plywood and the decoration generally was in a poor state. The lead roof was defective and allowing water to penetrate the building and the cross to the top of the tower had rotted. Illustrations 61, 62 and 63 show the tower before, during and after the recent restoration works. You will note the original louvres are now in view and a new gilded cross has been made.

Grace's *Guide to British Industrial History* explains that, in 1845 the bell

> was lodged in the tower prepared for its reception, and, upon trial, was found to be very satisfactory, its tone being much admired as solemn, melodious, and clear. It is from the Eagle Foundry of Mr. Sheridan, Church-street, Dublin, and is the No. 7 of a chime to which, last year, was awarded by the Royal Dublin Society, the prize of a gold medal of the value of ten guineas. Its diameter is 3 feet 10 inches, its weight 16 cwt. 1 qr. 12lbs.[33]

The *Liverpool Mercury* of that time comments:
> It is exceedingly gratifying to find that Irishmen are able to push a difficult, and, with us, a new branch of manufacture into a country where it has been long practised with power and success.

The recent restoration works to the bell tower provided us with the opportunity to access and inspect the bell chamber as can be seen in Illustration 58. On the bell it states that it was recast in 1951 by John Taylor & Co Founders, Loughborough who are still in existence.

---

[33]   See www.gracesguide.co.uk.

Within their archives is correspondence relating to this work. In a letter dated 17th August 1950 it states that a careful inspection was undertaken on 26th July, 1950, and established:

> The bell hangs in a precarious position, the ironwork which secures the headstock being so corroded that it is breaking away and it would be a wise precaution not to use the bell until it has received expert attention.
>
> The bell was cast in 1844, during a period which was a very poor one in the history of bell founding, and its tonal quality is very harsh and displeasing. Unfortunately, the shape of the bell and its thickness do not lend themselves to any appreciable improvement being brought about merely by the process of tuning; in order to make the bell into one of the rich and musical tone it will be necessary for it to be recast, when it would be entirely remodelled so that it could be tuned on our special "true-harmonic" system, which ensures great sweetness and purity of tone with maximum carrying power. In the process of recasting, the existing bell metal would be utilized again and sufficient new best quality bell metal added to compensate for wastage in melting, so that recast bell would weigh the same as at present.

The correspondence also highlights that originally the framework from which the bell was hung was part of the bell tower structure. As a result, when the bell was rung the whole structure incorporating the bell frame and tower would move. Taylors recommended that the bell should be hung rigid and provided with an electric motor which would be connected to a tolling hammer. This recommendation must have been accepted as this is the current arrangement.

The windows on both floors of the church have iron casements. The ground floor windows have segmental heads while the second storey windows are round headed. These windows are not thought to be original. An early photograph of the building suggests that there may once have been timber sliding sashes.

On three sides of the building there is green space, which is raised above the perimeter roads by a stone retaining wall. Along this retaining wall there are stretches of the original cast iron railings. At the two approaches from Park Road are classical stone gate piers; the northern one retains its original gates. On the south of the church the green space and pathways have been replaced with a tarmac surface.

The large size of the church interior is in some ways obscured by the galleries on three sides of the church and that fact the ground floor is sub-divided by the central confessional and sacristy areas added in 1985. The galleries themselves are supported on iron columns. They contain the original box pews and the organ. The organ is Listed in its own right and considered to be one of the earliest and finest instruments in the city. This organ, its casework probably designed by Slater himself, is discussed in more detail in Chapter 19.

The church interior has gone through three major changes since its construction. The first would have been the introduction of the high altar and reredos by the architect of Westminster Cathedral, John Francis Bentley in 1867. The altar was constructed with Staffordshire alabaster. It had a painted pieta to adorn the tomb beneath a mensa supported on marble columns. The reredos was sculpted in Caen stone with a domed canopy on the shoulders of two standing angels. The four moulded panels of the reredos contained heads of Abel, Noah, Abraham and Melchisedech, which were favourites with Bentley during this period. The images were painted, on slate, by Westlake. The walls either side of the reredos up to the great columns, were sheeted with vertical bands of Staffordshire alabaster, separated by narrow lines of green serpentine.

The high altar was approached by a flight of seven steps which curved around and outwards from the high altar. These steps were covered with oak and walnut parquetry by Waring & Gillow in 1905, at a cost of £125. Curved wooden communion rails fitted to the bottom step enclosed the sanctuary. An early twentieth century photograph of the Bentley high altar and sanctuary can be seen in Illustration 11.

In 1873 a Sacred Heart altar was installed halfway along the north wall of the church at a cost of £180. An altar dedicated to St Joseph was installed halfway along the south wall in 1891 at a cost of £247. The altar was by Boulton's of Cheltenham. Both the Sacred Heart and St Joseph altars were of brown veined marble, decorated in a post-gothic style, and both located at right angles to the side walls of the church.

The next major change occurred around 1953. Liverpool architect, Francis Xavier Velarde, was appointed to re-order the sanctuary. As part of this work the Bentley reredos was removed and the east wall between the great columns was sheeted in white travertine incorporating two mosaics patterns. The great columns were themselves painted white with gold banding. The Bentley altar was retained as were the communion rails. The parquetry to the steps appears to have been covered with white lino tiles in an attempt to protect the wood. Velarde introduced a new metal lectern and baptismal font. Whilst the lectern has now been replaced, the font remains in the south east corner, below the gallery. The crystal chandeliers, adjustable from above the ceiling, were also added at this time.

Photographs of the church taken around the time of the Velarde re-ordering show the altar with fine sculpted stone carving representing Christ teaching in the Temple. This is believed to have been added in the early twentieth century and replaced the previous painted pieta.

The final changes occurred in the mid 1980's and are largely what we see today. Prior to commencing this work half of the original communion rails had been removed to fit in with the changes in liturgical requirements. There was also a 'temporary' modern altar at the base of the steps and a plain wooden sedilia.

These changes were overseen by Liverpool architects Richard O'Mahoney & Partners. O'Mahoney himself had previously worked with Velarde. The work included constructing a new timber stud partition between the giant columns, in front of the Velarde travertine. The top of the new wall is finished with railed panels to match the gallery. Whilst the view is limited, behind the stud wall, Velarde's mosaic patterns and some travertine are still in place, as shown in Illustration 12.

The number of steps on the sanctuary was reduced to four and the Bentley altar was cut down to form the smaller square altar we see today. The altar was relocated to a newly created landing space on the second step.

A single storey sacristy block with lean to roof, was demolished at this time as it was considered structurally unsound. The sacristy block was located at the east end of the church and accessed via doors either side of the sanctuary. Drawings of the original sacristy block are shown in Illustrations 1, 2, 10 and 57. New sacristies were subsequently formed underneath the gallery alongside new confessionals. This split the ground floor space into two separate areas. To the east is the nave and to the west a parish meeting room with kitchen and toilet facilities. A few of the Stations of the Cross were located to the west end, and these were brought into the nave and fixed to the walls of the new sacristies and confessionals.

The Sacred Heart and St Joseph altars were also removed at this time. The relief of the Holy Family, in the north aisle under the gallery is thought to be from the St Joseph altar and some of the marble may also have been used to form the Tabernacle base in the South aisle.

Despite the changes that were made during the re-orderings of the 1950's and 1980's, the church still retains important original and early features that enhance the interior.

Probably the most impressive feature of the interior is the two great Corinthian columns to the sanctuary which support an elaborately decorated entablature. The capitals of the columns have acanthus leaf decoration which has been painted in gold leaf. The two large columns and the entablature frame a painting of the Crucifixion. This painting of 'Le Calvaire' dates from 1834 and is by the Flemish artist Nicaise de Keyser of Antwerp. De Keyser was a pupil of Jacob Jacobs and Mattheus Van Bree and became President of the Royal

Academy of Antwerp in 1855. Another of De Keyser's paintings, that of William II of Holland at the Battle of Waterloo, hangs in Windsor Castle. He received a semi-state funeral following his death in 1887.

The painting of 'Le Calvaire' measures 30ft. x 22ft. It is reported that it was cut down on either side before being put in position in 1835. Narrated elsewhere, the story behind the painting arriving at St Patrick's is that it was originally purchased by a Catholic church in Manchester; however, before the painting could be hung there, the church collapsed. Subsequently the painting was acquired by St Patrick's. It is without doubt a beautiful and significant work of art.

The last recorded restoration work on painting was in 1953, although we have found a specialist conservation report dated September 1993. Within the report it highlights that the painting at the time had suffered from crudely executed overpainting. It suggests that the overpainting was undertaken around the time of the 1950's restoration when the canvas was also maroufflaged to board. It appears that some surface cleaning, screw head treatment and the localised removal of overpainting to the figure of Mary Magdalen was undertaken in 1993. However, the report also makes recommendations for future treatment including the complete removal of all overpainting. It is unknown whether this has ever been implemented in whole or part and it may be beneficial for the parish to revisit this in the future with the aid of a conservation specialist.

In niches either side of the sanctuary at gallery level are statues of St Mark and St Matthew. They are thought to be original, older than the Stations of the Cross and the statues of St Patrick and Our Lady.

The church has a segmental arched ceiling which is panelled and decorated with Greek key ornament and foliated roundels.

Below the church is a crypt that extends approximately two-thirds of the way down the church. It is accessed via a set of original iron doors below the west gable.

Records show that between 1827 and 1841, 7466 people were buried in the crypt and the grounds of the church. There are a small number of vaults as you enter the crypt and a burial chamber behind another iron door with the inscription Peter Roberts. The crypt is divided into 6 bays. Within these bays appear to be pits that have been formed within the sandstone on which the church is built. It is thought that these may well be burial pits for the many people buried in the Crypt.

During our research we were able to find an early quinquennial inspection report for St Patrick's. By chance this dates from 1925 almost 100 years ago and around the time that the building would have been celebrating its first centenary. A copy of this report is provided within the appendix.

Today the church is not free from its building issues. Thanks to a grant provided by the DCMS and with the support of the Bishops' Conference, Historic England and the Archdiocese we have been able to undertake some much needed restoration work to the west gable, north aisle and transept. This work has addressed issues of water ingress and dry rot within the church. It has included the replacement of the capping sheet to the west gable wall, repointing to the west and north elevations, restoration of the bell tower, repairs to the roof, rainwater goods and below ground drainage. Internal damage caused by the dry rot outbreak including replastering replacing any damaged joinery and localised internal redecoration will also take place.

It is well noted that the whole of the interior would benefit from redecoration. There is however more work to be done before the full internal redecoration should be considered. This includes but is not limited to further repairs to areas of the roof, replacement/extensive repairs to the church windows, making good of the pathways and approaches to the church, reinstatement of the portico roof coverings, stone repairs, external plastering of the transepts and further investigative work into the crypt. At the time of writing this, the parish has gathered a dedicated group of volunteers who are actively looking to help with fundraising initiatives that will support future work at St Patrick's.

Appendix 1

Liverpool Mercury, **December 29, 1843**

TOTAL DESTRUCTION OF BRANCKER'S SUGAR
WAREHOUSE

Yesterday morning, about a quarter past 8 o'clock,
the extensive sugar-refining establishment of Mr
James Brancker (late Sir T. and J. Brancker) was
discovered to be on fire and so rapid was the
progress of the flames that in a few minutes the
whole range of buildings appeared to be one mass
of fire. Some idea of its rapidity may be formed
when we state that Mr Daniels of Lord-street, who
was looking out of his bedroom window at twelve
minutes past 8 o'clock saw no appearance of fire,
but on again looking towards the building, at
twenty minutes after eight, the whole appeared to
be in a blaze. In order that our readers may the
better understand the particulars we subjoin a
rough sketch of the ground plan.

Harrington-street, 125 feet

Farrer & Duckworth's warehouse

Passage about a yard wide and 182 feet

J. & H. Holmes's warehouse

Chimney ☐ shaft

Sugar warehouse, 8 stories
Destroyed

Sugar warehouse, 7 stories over the stove
Fire commenced
Destroyed

Sugar warehouse, 7 stories
Destroyed

Low shed

Purifying house, 4 stories
Destroyed

Warehouses

Molasses & water tanks
Destroyed

Chimney shaft ☐
Boiler shed
Destroyed

Engine house

Warehouses, 8 stories
Destroyed

Yard

Yard

Yard

Destroyed

Archway under w'house

W'house & office 5 stories

Charcoal w'house 5 stories

W'house 3 stories

House

Matthew-street

182 feet

Warehouses

From the above it will be seen that the premises extended from Harrington-street to Matthew-street, occupying an area of upwards of 4000 square yards. There are several buildings of different heights, the biggest being eight stories, and the range of windows across the three warehouses to the front of Harrington-street is ten in number; there is also in the same line a gateway which opens into the yard. There are, we understand, between 120 and 130 men constantly at work on the premises. They work, with the exception of a small apron in front, completely in a state of nudity and in an atmosphere varying from 120 to 130 degrees. It may be worthy of remark hear that, if we are correctly informed, the remuneration (which was some time ago 18s a week) for this severe labour was, up to the breaking out of the fire, only 16s. The fire, it appears, commenced in what is called the old stove-house, where the sugar undergoes the last process and is dried, and it is supposed it must have been smouldering there for the last day or two, during which, the men have felt that the atmosphere in the premises has been from ten to twelve degrees higher than usual. At the time the fire occurred, the greater part of the men were lying upon the floor resting themselves, it being the breakfast hour, and the first intimation they received of it was from a shout which ran generally through the building: "Men, save your lives; The place is on fire." As might naturally be expected, the men were thrown into a state of great excitement, and their fears were increased, when on looking out from the top stories, they saw the flames and smoke bursting forth with intense fury. Those in the lower parts of the buildings managed to escape without much difficulty but those who were unfortunately situated at the top of the premises fared considerably worse. They ran to the staircase, but found there was no escape in that direction, in consequence of the volumes of smoke which were making their way upwards, and in their agony of despair, they rushed to the windows and called for aid. In the mean time the alarm of fire had reached the fire-police station, situated a very short distance from the place, and an engine was immediately got out and conveyed to Matthew-street. Perceiving the imminent danger of the men, Mr Hewitt returned to the station, and with the assistance of his brother and other men, brought ladders to the rescue of poor fellows who were standing on the outside of the building in a state of nakedness, amidst dense masses of smoke, momentarily expecting to be consumed by the raging fire beneath them, which was every instant increasing. One of the hands, named Cornelius, a man upwards of 60 years of age, managed to slide down a rope, and thereby escaped. Several at the Mathew-street end contrived to descend by a ladder which was raised against the building, and reached the ground unhurt. In Harrington-street one of the ladders, on being raised, snapped near the top, and was for some time rendered useless. At this period there were between 30 and 40 men in the street, and although it is mournful to relate such an instance of inhumanity, yet it is the fact, that they refused to render any assistance to the parties who were endeavouring to raise the ladder upon a lorry, so as to make it long enough to reach the poor fellows above. This object, however, being accomplished, one of the men (George White) attempted to reach the ladder, which he could barely touch with his feet, and whether from his state of anxiety, the heat of the place, or being blinded by the smoke, he loosed his hold, and was precipitated to the bottom. In his descent he fell upon a man who was assisting to hold the ladder, and both were removed apparently in a lifeless state. Poor White was conveyed along North John-street, to the Northern Hospital, in a naked state, his body presenting a most appalling sight. Thomas Jones, the foreman of the melting gang, finding escape otherwise hopeless, slided down by means of the water-pipe, which was fastened perpendicularly to the wall. The pipe at the time, in many places, was nearly red hot and the state of the poor man's hands when he reached the street, in a much exhausted state, may be more easily conceived than described. Scarce a particle of flesh remained upon them, and his sufferings were intense for a time. After getting them dressed, however, he was to be seen walking up and down the streets, as unconcerned, apparently, as the least interested spectator. Three of the men, named Britton, O'Hare, and Hugh Jones, were in the sixth story of the eastern warehouse, in Harrington-street, and when the alarm reached them they made every effort to retreat by the staircase, but were unable to do so. Foiled in their efforts, they became desperate, and leaped from one of the windows to the top of the purifying-house. Here they narrowly escaped suffocation from the thick dark masses of gaseous matter which was bursting out upon them. They fell on their faces on the roof, and were, with considerable difficulty, rescued by Mr Hewitt, assisted by one of the workmen, named Gerard Brice, who placed ladder within their reach. One of the gangs who were busy papering the goods in the top story first became aware of the fire, by seeing the smoke issuing from the yard. Four of them immediately rushed forward to reach the staircase. James Corregan fell in his progress. He got upon the roof of the warehouse, in the hope of jumping upon the one adjoining, belonging to Messrs Holmes and Sons, but finding that much higher he was thus baffled in his attempt to escape. He was about to throw himself into the street, when he was observed from below, and advised not to do so. He then retreated into the sugar-house again, got through the window, made a jump to the spout, and slided down by it. The spout was not warm, and the only injury received by the man, who was naked, was occasioned by the friction of the pipe against his breast. Joseph Price followed this example, and escaped unhurt. Peter Canter had his head much singed as he made his way to the ladder by which he escaped. About half a dozen made their way to the bottom of the building, through the pulley-hole, and one poor fellow, Hugh Roberts, mistook it for the staircase, fell down, and was much hurt. The ladder placed to reach Patrick Martin did not reach the place where he was standing by two stories and the poor fellow, in his eagerness to escape, jumped down towards it. He seized it and descended by it to the ground, but in the fall he struck against the ladder, and severely injured his side. Thomas Garland escaped by means of the pulley hole, and rolled into the street naked, and almost frantic. At length a sheet was given to him, with this he covered his nakedness and shortly afterwards was induced to return home. Mr Bickley warehouseman to Messrs Crosfield, and his men, as also the men belonging to the establishment of Mr Sharpe, rendered efficient service in saving the lives of the poor men who were placed in such awful situations.

The scene, at this time, in Harrington-street and Matthew-street was of the most heart-rending and appalling nature. Men, who had just themselves been rescued, were running about naked, bewailing, in a half frantic manner, the pending fate of their fellow labourers, and crying in the wildest manner for help. Women and children were searching for a husband or a parent, whom they could not recognise, even when found, in consequence of their disfigurement, and despair seemed to have taken possession of every countenance.

Most of the men were cut by the glass in making their way through the windows, and, with scarcely an exception, they have lost all their clothing. This, with the loss of their employment will, we fear, make them great sufferers by this lamentable occurrence.

We have before mentioned that the fire was first discovered in the old stove-house, which is near the centre of the premises, immediately below the sugar warehouse, and near the large chimney in the centre. As soon as it was perceived, a message was sent to James Doyle the excise officer, to open the stove door, whilst a messenger was despatched to acquaint Mr J Brancker of the calamity. He was coming down Duke-street, on his way to the office at the time the lamentable intelligence was communicated to him. But a few minutes elapsed after the opening of the stove door before the fire extended the whole length of the building. The flames spread completely along the warehouse running from the one street to the other, and also up Harrington-street as far as the low shed. For a short time only they were confined to the centre stories, from the windows and doors of which the volumes of flame roared with intense fury. No doubt the rapidity with which the fire spread and communicated to every part of the building may be accounted for by this circumstance:– The racks upon which the sugar cases rested were made entirely of wood, and the heat of the place and the oily nature of the substances with which they came in contact, rendered them particularly inflammable,—so much so, indeed, that if the building had been fired in fifty different places, the bursting out of the flames could scarcely have been more simultaneous.

Before nine o'clock several of the engines were got into play, and there was a good supply of water in the mains. In order the more efficiently to reach this, the street was broken up, and the hose from the engines placed in the opening, so that the water was supplied in great abundance. By this time, however, the flames in the sugar-house had completely enveloped the whole building, and Mr Whitty at once saw that the only way in which the exertions of the fire police could be advantageously directed was in the preservation of the adjoining property. The premises were only separated on the east side by a narrow passage, little more than a yard wide from a stupendous pile of warehouses, the property of Messrs Henry Holmes and Sons, and the warehouse of Messrs Farrer and Duckworth. At the west end, at some little distance from the sugar-house, Harvey's warehouse was situated. On the south side, besides one or two small cottages, there were a number of warehouses, separated only by the width of Harrington-street whilst, on the north side, a large number of small houses, many of them the residences of the workmen, were cut off from the flames by Matthew-street. Fortunately there was little or no wind at the time, but what there was came from the west. Had there been anything like the breezes which generally prevail at this season of the year, no human exertions could have saved the warehouses on the south side of Harrington-street, and with them, part of the north side of Lord-street must also have been destroyed. Already had the wood-work outside the small cottage immediately fronting the sugar-house taken fire, but it was speedily extinguished; and then the branch was directed towards the wooden cat-head at the top of the warehouse adjoining, which showed symptoms of early ignition, from the intense heat with which it was in contact. Again, on the west side, the branches of a couple of engines were turned towards Harvey's warehouses, and, as the fire progressed, this was found to be one of the most useful precautionary measures, for by it the flames were prevented from reaching the warehouse, which was stocked with cotton, coffee, and other valuable articles. The steam which arose, when the water was thrown upon the walls, was evidence sufficient of the danger of the building, from its proximity to the scene of conflagration.

The next point to which the efforts of the fire men were directed, was the warehouse of Messrs H. Holmes and Sons. It is somewhat remarkable, that at the time of the erection of the sugar warehouse, a suggestion was made to do away with the passage between the warehouse and the sugar-house. This the Messrs Holmes fortunately resisted, and had they not done so, their magnificent piles of warehouses would now have been burnt to the ground, for, had these adjoined the sugar-house, filled as they are, with cotton and general merchandise, nothing could have saved them. It was also a fortunate circumstance that they presented entirely a dead wall to the passage so that the fire could obtain no hold without first penetrating the bricks and mortar. Hose having been carried up the building, a couple of engines were continually employed pouring water upon the walls and by these means the property was preserved. An engine was stationed in Matthew-street, for the purpose of preserving the property opposite, and when not occupied in playing upon the wood-work of the houses, rendered efficient service on the other side of the street. The top stories of the building marked 'charcoal house' in the plan, was used as a warehouse, and in it Mr James Brancker had deposited a large number of valuable paintings, which he had removed on his leaving his late residence at Ambleside. The roof of this place having ignited, Mr Samuel Holme rushed into the upper stories, and, by his personal and praiseworthy exertions, not only were the pictures removed and placed in safety, but the building itself, and the cottages and manager's house adjoining, preserved. Whilst the fire police and those in authority were thus dividing their exertions to check the progress of the devouring element, the occupiers of Harvey's warehouse employed men to remove their property, and their example was followed by Messrs Donnell and Appleby, cheese factors, who caused to be removed a vast number of cheese, and a large quantity of flour in sacks. Occupiers of warehouses in Rainford-gardens, North John-street, and Matthew-street, partook in the general alarm, and removed their goods, thereby incurring considerable loss and trouble.

This being the state of affairs on the outskirts of the fire, we turn our attention now to the conflagration itself. The flames continued to extend and increase in magnitude until the whole of that part described in the plan as destroyed was one sheet of fire. Passing into the yard the site was one of the most awful yet magnificent, appalling yet sublime, we ever remember to have witnessed. From upwards of 100 windows the flames were bursting forth with fearful intensity. Each story seemed like a blazing avenue extending from one end of the building to the other, the consuming timbers were cracking with a loud noise, and the machinery was falling with tremendous crashes into the cellars beneath. About half-past nine, what are called the 'blow pans' fell from the fourth story. On the instant a loud explosion was heard, and the roof of the centre warehouse in Harrington-street fell in. As soon as the materials reached the bottom of the building, the flames burst out with a noise resembling the roaring of a mighty hurricane, and immense volumes of fire ascended nearly 100 feet above the warehouse. Shortly afterwards a similar effect was witnessed at the falling in of the roof nearest Matthew-street. Story after story gave way, until, at about half-past ten, it began to be apparent that the fire would not extend beyond its limits at that time.

From the quantity of water thrown on the building, the streets, especially inside the yard, were completely deluged with a liquid resembling thin molasses, and in some places the sugar was seen in a crusted or toffee state. Considerable quantities of the former were collected in barrels. Molten lead ran from the roofs down the sides of the buildings, and even iron itself was melted by the intense heat.

About a quarter to one o'clock the gable end fronting Matthew-street gave way, but fortunately, although a portion of the materials fell outwards, no one was injured.

The premises were supplied with a large reservoir of water, and every precaution taken for the purpose of suppressing the fire. An engine for pumping water from the reservoir was on the premises. It connected with, and was worked by the steam engine. Large connecting pipes ran up every building, and smaller pipes branched off to each room, in order that every story might immediately be flooded with water, but so rapidly did the flames spread, that there was not even time to connect the engine before it was rendered useless.

In what terms shall we notice the efforts of Mr Whitty and the officers under him, in the preservation of the surrounding property? What language can convey, to those who did not witness them, any idea of their superhuman, we had almost said, exertions? Sure we are, there is nowhere a set of men more to be praised for manly daring and intrepidity. Their successful efforts yesterday are beyond all praise, and we hope the Fire Committee will see fit to grant them rewards somewhat commensurate with their labour. Mr Hewitt was early on the spot with the engines, which were in capital order, and soon brought into play. He was foremost in the post of danger, and urged, by his example, the officers of the Fire Police to the willing performance of their duties. No less active and energetic was his brother, Mr G. Hewitt, whose exertions on all occasions deserve especial notice. Superintendents Leverett, Brown, and Macdonald were on the ground soon after the fire broke out, and to their superior arrangements is to be attributed the saving of a large quantity of property, and the excellent order which was preserved. His Worship the Mayor arrived a little before ten, and expressed great anxiety as to the fate of the property. Mr James Lawrence, the chairman of the Fire Committee, attended, and, by his judicious advice, assisted in the general arrangements. Many of the Common Council and leading gentlemen of the town visited the conflagration during the day, and Sir Thomas Brancker and Mr James Brancker were on the ground till evening.

We have been favoured with the following notes as to the cases received at the Northern Hospital:—

George White, severe injury of the head and spine, with fracture of the left arm—in a very dangerous state, and scarcely expected to recover. Patrick Cassidy wound of the temple, with concussion of the brain. Hugh Jones, severe burns of the arms, head, and chest; the two last, though severely injured, are likely to do well. One man was taken to the Infirmary, but he is only slightly injured.

The reports as to the number of lives lost vary, from five to nine. Some imagine that, from the number of men seen at the windows, even more should have perished, but of course it is impossible, at this early period, to ascertain this fact correctly. We have been furnished with the names of the following men, who are at present missing:- Robert Woods, Thomas Tyrer and —- Jinling.

One of the fireman was severely hurt by a kick from one of the engine horses, and another had his hand and wrist much cut with the glass in one of the windows.

The loss sustained, including the buildings, machinery, goods, &c is estimated under £70,000. A considerable portion of this is insured. So far as we can learn, the following are the sums underwritten by the various offices:-

Phoenix, £800; Liverpool, 3000; Alliance, 4000; Yorkshire, 3000; West of England, 3000; London, 2000; Sun, 5000; Imperial, 3000; North British, 500; Scottish Union, 3000; total 32,500.

There is one curious circumstance connected with the fire. Many of the streets and yards in a north-east direction from the scene of the conflagration were thickly strewn with a white substance resembling a thin flake of lime, or what falls sometimes from ceilings often whitewashed, it extended along Whitechapel, Byrom-street, and in the higher streets, from St Anne's and Soho-streets up to Everton. It is too heavy to be burnt paper, and so little lime is used that it cannot be that substance nor is it like charred timber. Whether sugar, by the intensity of the heat, could be sublimed to such a substance, our informant could not say.

Ten o'clock

We have just returned from the scene of the conflagration, and find it is now completely subdued. With the exception of a little light escaping from the extreme eastern warehouse in Harrington-street, the whole is now a vast mass of black smouldering ruins. Three engines only are playing, and but few persons are near the place. There still remain doubts as to the precise loss of life.

A rumour has just reached us that the remains of one of the poor fellows have been discovered in the ruins. There can be little probability of the truth of such a rumour, for considering the intensity of the fire, it is next to impossible that any traces of those who have been burned will ever be found.

APPENDIX 2

THE DEANERY OF ST CHARLES, LIVERPOOL

REPORT OF THE INSPECTION OF THE

MISSION OF ST. PATRICK.

MADE DECEMBER 9th, 1925

A) CHURCH

(1) EXTERIOR

a) BOUNDARY WALLS require pointing in places.

b) GATES & RAILINGS, were painted in 1924.

c) SPOUTS & GUTTERS, were painted in 1924. but many are in a sad state of repair.

d) FRONT WALLS OF THE CHURCH, require pointing.

e) DOORS require painting again.

f) VENTILATORS, require attention.

g) DRAINS are in good order.

h) THE FLAGS, in the church yard are very uneven.

i) WOODWORK OF WINDOWS, is rotten & needs replacing.

(2) INTERIOR

a) FLOORS in good condition.

b) BENCHES, some require varnishing. All the woodwork will be painted next year.

c) WALLS & CEILINGS, have been recently painted. The Walls of THE GALLERY will be painted next year.

d) CONFESSIONALS, require painting. No Crucifix in two of them.

e) FONT is clean and all requisites for Baptism are kept in a locked cupboard. HOLY-OIL STOCKS, are not over clean and require polishing. The GATES & RAILS around the Baptistry are nicely painted. The gate kept locked. STONE OF THE FONT, requires restoring.

f) THE SANCTUARY

   f.1 HIGH ALTAR is well kept.

   f.2 TABERNACLE. White silk curtains within, are much soiled & unfit for use. Outer curtains in good repair.

   f.3 HIGH ALTAR CERE-CLOTH is worn out, & should be replaced.

   f.4 CARPETS. Sanctuary carpets & rugs are in fairly good condition, but worn.

   f.5 FURNITURE. All the furniture on the Sanctuary is in good repair.

   f.6 CANDLESTICKS. ALL, as well as the Vases have been recently re-lacquered.

   f.7 ST JOSEPH'S ALTAR. in Alabaster is clean & has a good carpet.

f.8 SACRED HEART ALTAR. is clean & has a good carpet.

(B) THE SACRISTY

a) Well furnished with VESTING-TABLE, & WARDROBES. All clean & in good condition.

b) WORKING-SACRISTY, requires cleaning & painting.

c) SACRED VESSELS. FOUR CHALICES & TWO CIBORIA in good condition.

d) TWO REMONSTRANCES, one requires resilvering.

e) ASPERGES BOWL requires re-lacquering.

f) VESTMENTS. One white vestment is soiled & unfit for use. THREE PURPLE vestments soiled & unfit for use. TWO WHITE COPES require cleaning. ONE COPE is past repair & cleaning. ALBS, COPES, COTTAS & LINEN are well preserved & kept in their respective drawers.

g) The INVENTORY of the contents of the Sacristy has been checked and found correct.

(C) THE PRESBYTERY

(1) EXTERIOR

a) WALLS in places need re-pointing.

b) SPOUTS—recently repainted.

c) WINDOW FRAMES. recently re-painted.

d) DRAINS in good order.

(2) INTERIOR

a) WALLS & CEILINGS, painted & papered a few years ago.

b) CARPETS are rather worn.

c) TWO BED-ROOMS used by curates on the top landing are in a poor condition. The MANTELS are rusty & GRATES old & useless. CARPETS are worn out. Rooms poorly furnished. Rain comes through the ceilings.

d) The INVENTORY of all the FURNITURE, SILVER, CROCKERY & HOUSEHOLD EFFECTS has been examined & found correct.

(D) MISSION BOOKS

a) BAPTISMAL REGISTER. All the Baptisms are correctly entered with the exception of a few omissions of names.

b) MARRIAGE REGISTER. All marriages are most carefully entered except a few names omitted.

c) CONFIRMATION REGISTER. All entries correct.

d) MASS BOOK.

d.1 No FOUNDATION MASSES.

d.2 MANUAL. All Masses entered with care, giving dates of reception & fulfilment.

(E) THE SCHOOLS

a) The schools have been condemned & will only be recognised after extensive alterations.

b) DRAINS are in good order.

c) SPOUTS, WINDOWS & RAILINGS painted in 1924.

(F) THE RECTORS WILL

The WILL was produced and is signed by the REV. M. TIMMONS & duly witnessed. The EXECUTORS are two Priests.

R. Blanchard

BIBLIOGRAPHY

Archdiocese of Liverpool Directory.

Bance, S. *The Hospital and Cemetery of Ireland: The Irish and Disease in Nineteenth Century Liverpool.* University of Warwick Centre for the History of Medicine, 2014.

Belchem, J. *Irish, Catholic and Scouse.* Liverpool University Press, 2007.

Bennett, J. Canon. *Fr Nugent of Liverpool.* Liverpool Catholic Children's Protection Society, 1949.

Burke, T. *Catholic History of Liverpool.* Tinling, 1910.

Catholic Directory of England and Wales.

De L'Hopital, W. *Westminster Cathedral and Its Architect.* New York: Dodd, Mead and Co., 1919.

Doyle, P. *Mitres and Missions in Lancashire: A History of the Roman Catholic Diocese of Liverpool, 1850–2000.* Bluecoat Press, 2005.

Doyle, P. *The Correspondence of Alexander Goss, Bishop of Liverpool 1856–1872.* Boydell Press, 2014.

Dublin Morning Post, 11th March, 1824.

Dudley, R. *Fire Insurance in Dublin, 1700–1860.* Irish Economic and Social History Vol 30, pp 24–51, Sage Publications, 2003.

Elvin, L. *Bishop and Son, Organ Builders.* Elvin, 1984

Furnival, J. & Knowles, A. *Archbishop Derek Worlock—His Personal Journey.* Chapman, 1998.

Goethals, E. *Gleanings from the History of St Patrick's, Liverpool.* 1911.

Grace's Guide to British Industrial History.

Hocter, A. J. *St Patrick's 150th Anniversary Souvenir.* 1978.

Irish Post, 21st May, 2018

Lewis, D. *The Churches of Liverpool.* Bluecoat Press, 2001.

Liverpool Archdiocesan Archives: Original Documents, St Patrick's Church.

Liverpool Mercury, as dated in text.

Liverpool Record Office: Brancker Archive

Longley, C. *The Worlock Archive.* Chapman, 2000.

McCarren, M. C. Trotman, F., Piggin, M. *With Devotedness and Love 1844–1994.* F. C. J., 1994.

Midwinter, E. *Old Liverpool.* David & Charles, 1971.

Muir, R. *History of Liverpool.* Liverpool University Press / Williams & Norgate, London, 1907.

Muir, T. E. *Roman Catholic Church Music in England 1791–1914.* Routledge, 2016.

Norman, D. & Erdos, G. *Families without Fatherhood.* I. E. A., 1992.

O'Connor, P. Rev. *I Met a Miracle.* Catholic Truth Society, 1973.

O'Neill, M. *St Anthony's, Scotland Road, Liverpool.* Gracewing, 2010.

Plumb, B. *Arundel to Zabi.* North West Catholic History Society, 2nd Edition, 2006.

Plumb, B. *Found Worthy.* North West Catholic History Society, 1986.

Pooley, C. 'Living in Liverpool: The Modern City'. In: Belchem, J. (Ed), *Liverpool 800 : Culture, Character and History.* Liverpool University Press, 2006.

Saunders Newsletter Dublin, 5th October; 9th October 20th October and 18th November, 1824.

Sharples, J. *Liverpool.* Yale University Press, 2004.

Souvenir of St Patrick's Bazaar, 1923.

St Patrick's Centenary Souvenir Programme. 1827–1927.

St Patrick's School Log Book.

Stonehouse. J. *Pictorial Liverpool: Its Annals; Commerce; Shipping; Institutions; Public Buildings; &c: A New and Complete Handbook for Resident, Visitor and Tourist.* Liverpool: H. Lacey, 1844.

Waring, C. Rev. Churches In and Around Liverpool. Cathedral Record, January 1947.

ILLUSTRATIONS

1. Ordnance Survey of Liverpool, 1849.

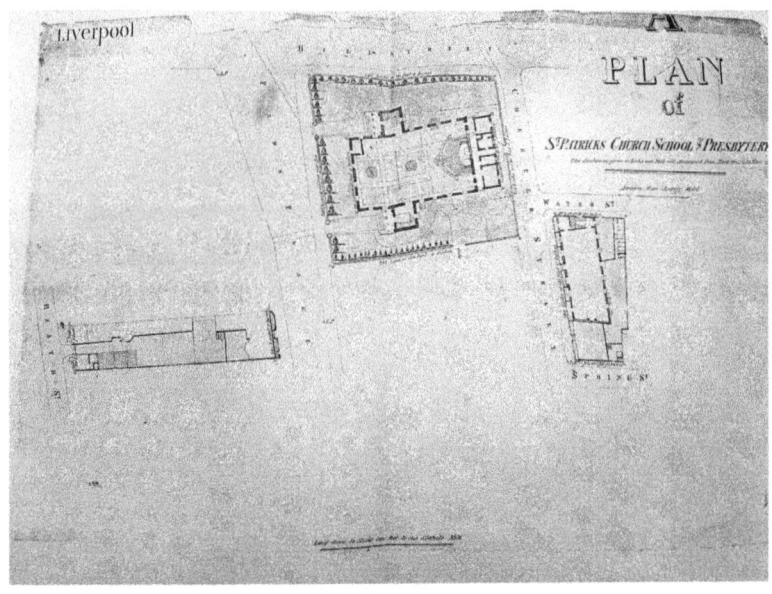

2. St Patrick's Church, School and Presbytery, 1844 Survey.

3. Wesley's Chapel, Stanhope Street: Payne, 1829.

4. St Patrick's Chapel, Toxteth Park, Liverpool: West Front, 1828.

COPY OF THE LEASE OF SAINT PATRICK'S CHAPEL.

This Indenture, made the eighteenth day of MAY, in the Year of our Lord One Thousand Eight Hundred and Twenty-nine BETWEEN Alexander Ryan, of Harrington, near Liverpool, in the County of LANCASTER, Lime Burner; Matthew Connor, of Liverpool aforesaid, Trunkmaker; Joseph Birdsall, of Liverpool aforesaid, Druggist; William Baynes, of Harrington aforesaid, Joiner; the Reverend John Walker, of Harrington aforesaid, Clerk; and the Reverend Francis Murphy, of the same place, Clerk; *of the one part* AND the Right Reverend Thomas Penswick, of Liverpool aforesaid, Doctor of Divinity; Thomas Sherburn, of the Willows, near Kirkham, in the said County, Clerk; Thomas Pennington, of Orrell Mount, in the said County, Clerk; Henry Gillow, of Appleton, in the said County, Clerk; and John Parsons, of Manchester, in the said County, Clerk; *of the other part:* WITNESSETH, THAT for and in consideration of the sum of Two Thousand Pounds of lawful money of Great Britain by the said Thomas Penswick, Thomas Sherburn, Thomas Pennington, Henry Gillow, and John Parsons, to the said Alexander Ryan, Matthew Connor, Joseph Birdsall, William Baynes, John Walker, and Francis Murphy, in hand well and truly paid upon or immediately before the execution hereof, the receipt whereof THEY the said Alexander Ryan, Matthew Connor, Joseph Birdsall, William Baynes, John Walker, and Francis Murphy, DO HEREBY ACKNOWLEDGE, and from the same and every part thereof DO hereby acquit, release, and for ever discharge the said Thomas Penswick, Thomas Sherburn, Thomas Pennington, Henry Gillow, and John Parsons, their executors, administrators, and assigns, and every of them for ever by these presents; AND also in consideration of the rent, covenants, and agreements hereinafter reserved and contained on the part and behalf of the said Thomas Penswick, Thomas Sherburn, Thomas Pennington, Henry Gillow, and John Parsons, their executors, administrators, and assigns, to be paid, kept, observed, and performed THEY the said Alexander Ryan, Matthew Connor, Joseph Birdsall, William Baynes, John Walker, and Francis Murphy have and each of them hath demised, leased, and to farm let, and by these presents do and each of them doth demise, lease, and to farm let, unto the said Thomas Penswick, Thomas Sherburn, Thomas Pennington, Henry Gillow, and John Parsons, their executors, administrators, and assigns ALL THAT PIECE OR PARCEL OF LAND OR GROUND, situate and being on the East side of PARK PLACE, in TOXTETH PARK, in the Parish of Walton-on-the-Hill, in the said County of LANCASTER, containing in front thereto fifty-four yards and two feet, and in breadth at the back forty-five yards and two feet and three inches, and running in rear or depth backwards on the South side, fifty-three yards two feet and nine inches, and on the North side fifty-four yards two feet and eleven inches, and containing in the whole 2711½ superficial square yards of land, or thereabouts, be the several dimensions thereof more or less; bounded on the North by Upper Hill Street, on the South by land belonging to Doctor John Hughes and Mr. Robinson, on the East by a Street of ten yards wide, called Chester Street, and on the West by Park Place aforesaid TOGETHER with the Chapel or Building, and all and singular other the erections or buildings thereon, and TOGETHER with all and singular houses, outhouses, edifices, buildings, yards, ways, water-courses, easements, privileges, profits, commodities, advantages, hereditaments, and appurtenances whatsoever to the said Piece of Land, Chapel, Building, Hereditaments, and Premises, belonging or in any wise appertaining EXCEPT AND ALWAYS RESERVED OUT OF THIS PRESENT DEMISE, FULL AND FREE LIBERTY FOR ALL AND EVERY PERSONS WHOMSOEVER TO USE AND OCCUPY THE GROUND FLOOR OF THE SAID CHAPEL OR BUILDING, BEING OF THE DIMENSIONS FOLLOWING: THAT IS TO SAY, SIXTY-NINE FEET FROM THE WESTWARDLY WALL, RUNNING EASTWARDLY; AND SIXTY FEET FROM NORTH TO SOUTH, AT ALL PROPER TIMES AND SEASONS, FOR THE PURPOSE OF DIVINE WORSHIP ONLY; AND WITH FULL AND FREE LIBERTY OF INGRESS, EGRESS, AND REGRESS, INTO, OVER, AND THROUGH THE YARD OR BURIAL-GROUND ATTACHED TO AND ADJOINING THE SAID CHAPEL AND BUILDING, FOR THE PURPOSE OF GOING TO AND RETURNING FROM THE SAME: BUT FOR THE PURPOSE ABOVE MENTIONED ONLY ....
TO HAVE AND TO HOLD the said Piece or Parcel of Land or Ground, Chapel, Building, and Hereditaments, and all and singular other the Premises hereby demised, or intended so to be, with all and every of the rights, privileges, and appurtenances to the same Premises or any part thereof, belonging (EXCEPT AS HEREIN BEFORE EXCEPTED) UNTO the said Thomas Penswick, Thomas Sherburn, Thomas Pennington, Henry Gillow, and John Parsons, their executors, administrators, and assigns, from the day of the date of these presents, for and during the full and complete term of FIVE THOUSAND YEARS thence next ensuing YIELDING AND PAYING for the same, yearly and every year, during the said term, UNTO the said Alexander Ryan, Matthew Connor, Joseph Birdsall, William Baynes, John Walker, and Francis Murphy, their heirs and assigns, the rent of a pepper-corn, if demanded, on the last day of each year AND the said Thomas Penswick, Thomas Sherburn, Thomas Pennington, Henry Gillow, and John Parsons, do hereby for themselves jointly and severally, and for their several and respective heirs, executors, administrators, and assigns, *covenant, promise, and agree,* to and with the said Alexander Ryan, Matthew Connor, Joseph Birdsall, William Baynes, John Walker, and Francis Murphy, their heirs and assigns, in manner following: THAT IS TO SAY, THAT they the said Thomas Penswick, Thomas Sherburn, Thomas Pennington, Henry Gillow, and John Parsons, shall and will at all times, and from time to time, during the continuance of the term hereby demised, well and substantially repair, and keep repaired, at his and their own expense and costs, all and singular the inner parts of the said demised premises, and also all and singular the outside brick-work, plastering, slating, tiling, railing, and other outer parts of the same Chapel, Building, and Premises .... AND SHALL AND WILL, DURING THE SAID TERM, KEEP AND PRESERVE THE INSCRIPTION* ENGRAVED UPON STONE, AND FIXED IN THE OUTWARD WALL IN THE WEST FRONT OF THE SAID CHAPEL, IN AS GOOD A STATE OF PRESERVATION AS THE SAME NOW IS, AND SHALL NOT NOR WILL ALLOW THE SAME TO BE REMOVED, ALTERED, OR DAMAGED IN ANY WISE HOWSOEVER .... AND shall and will, during the continuance of the said term, keep the said Chapel or Building and Premises insured against loss from accidents from fire in some reputable Office of Insurance AND FURTHER, that they, the said Thomas Penswick, Thomas Sherburn, Thomas Pennington, Henry Gillow, and John Parsons, their executors, administrators, and assigns, shall not, nor will, at any time hereafter convert the said Chapel into any other building, or suffer the same to be used for any other purpose than as a place of Divine Worship according to the rites and doctrine of the Roman Catholic Church AND ALSO that they the said Thomas Penswick, Thomas Sherburn, Thomas Pennington, Henry Gillow, and John Parsons, their executors, administrators, or assigns, shall not, nor will, during the said term, demise, let, assign, set over, or otherwise part with the said Premises, or any part thereof, to any person, or any estate, term, or interest therein, unto any person or persons whomsoever than Clergymen of the Roman Catholic Church AND the said Alexander Ryan, Matthew Connor, Joseph Birdsall, William Baynes, John Walker, and Francis Murphy, for themselves, jointly and severally, and for their several and respective heirs, executors, and administrators, do hereby covenant, promise, and agree to and with the said Thomas Penswick, Thomas Sherburn, Thomas Pennington, Henry Gillow, and John Parsons, their executors, administrators, and assigns (performing and observing the several covenants and agreements hereinbefore contained on their or any of their part, to be observed or performed) shall and lawfully may peaceably and quietly have, hold, use, occupy, possess, and enjoy the said piece or parcel of Land, Chapel or Building, and Premises, hereby demised or otherwise assured or intended so to be, with the rights, members, and appurtenances to the same belonging, for and during the said term of Five Thousand Years expressed or intended so to be hereby granted thereof, without any lawful or rightful hindrance, molestation, or disturbance whatsoever of or by them the said Alexander Ryan, Matthew Connor, Joseph Birdsall, William Baynes, John Walker, and Francis Murphy, or any of their heirs or assigns, or any other person or persons whomsoever IN WITNESS WHEREOF, the said parties have hereunto set their names and seals, the day and year first above written

* * SAINT PATRICK'S CHAPEL,
" Built by Public Subscription, under the express stipulation that the whole of the Ground Floor should for ever Remain Free for the Accommodation of ALL. " Began A.D. 1821.] " Keep therefore the words of this Covenant, and fulfil them."—Deut. xxix. 9. [Finished A.D. ."

5.   St Patrick's Church Lease.

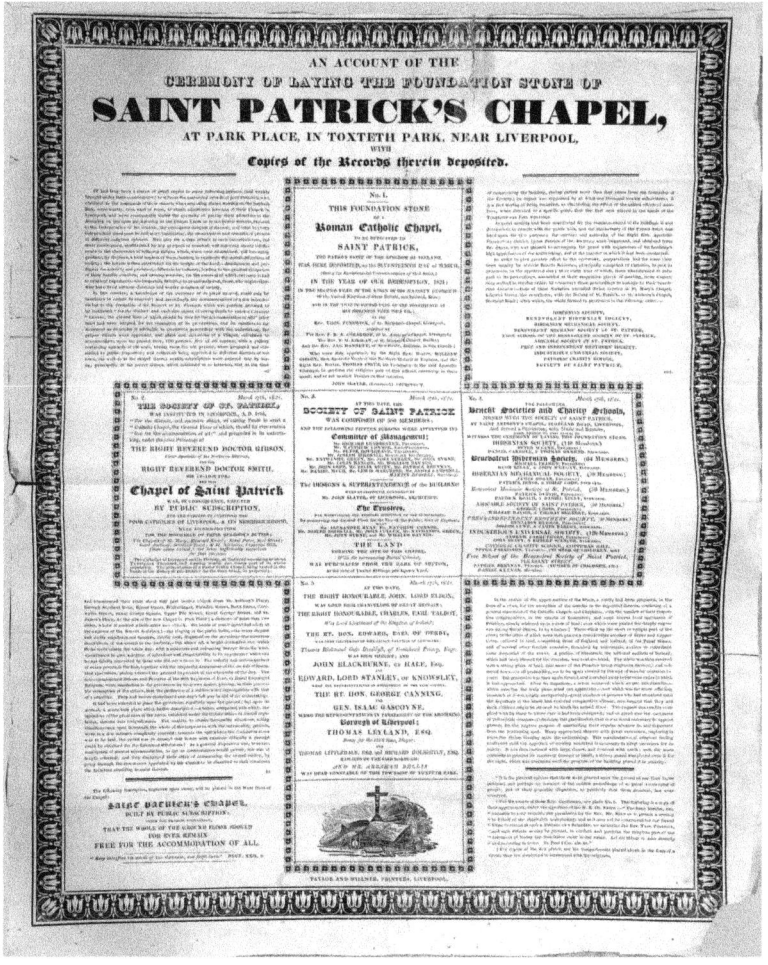

6. St Patrick's Foundation Record, 1821.

7. Fr Francis Murphy, 1827–1837.

8. Fr John Walker, 1827–1830.

9. Slater's Sanctuary Design: Elevation and Ground Plan, 1827.

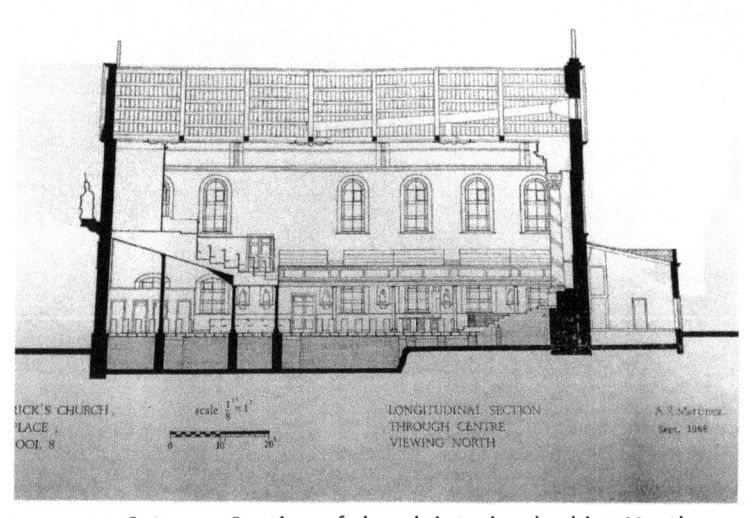

10. Cutaway Section of church interior, looking North.
Before 1986.

11. High Altar, J. F. Bentley, 1867.

12. *High Altar, modified by F. X. Velarde with first reordering,*
before 1986.

13. *High Altar radically reordered, March 1986.*

14. High Altar, 2020.

15. St Patrick's Church, NW View, 1898–1910.

16. Memorial Cross, 1898.

17. Organ Case in West Gallery, 2020.

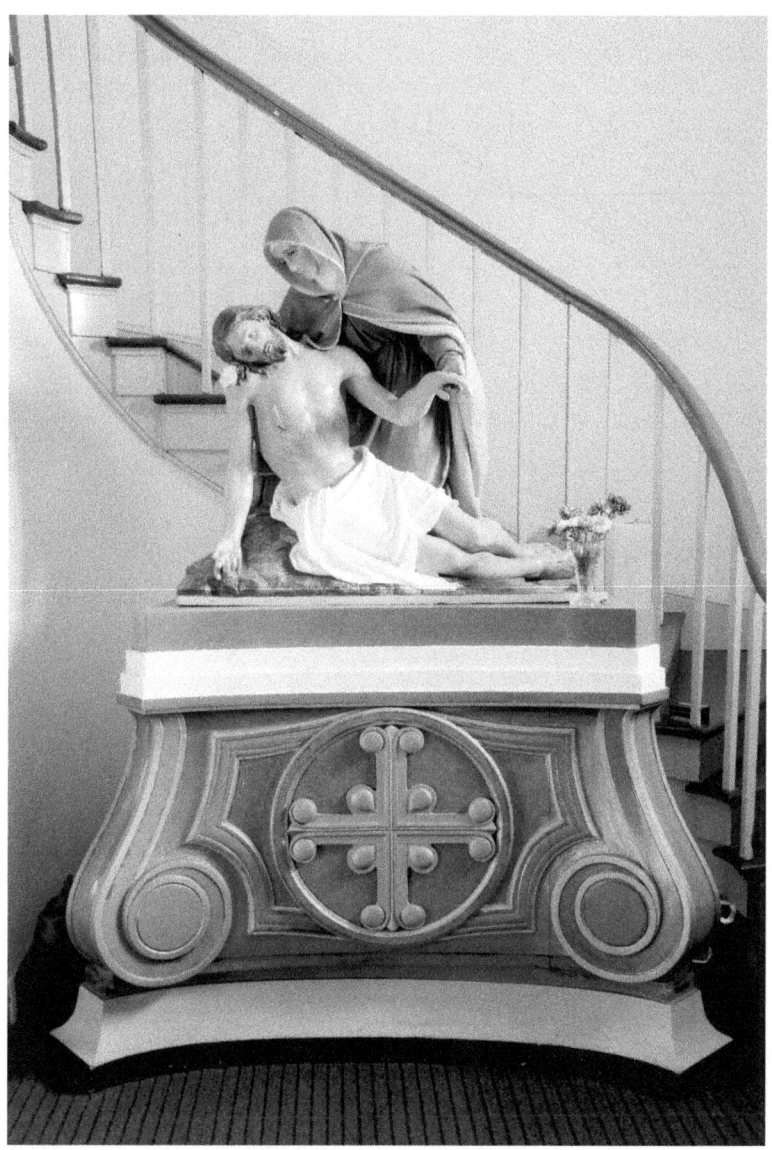

18. Pieta in church porch.

19. St Patrick's statue in church porch.

20. Presbytery, 2020.

21. Canon Goethals Memorial Hall and Schools, 1928.

22. *Peter Roberts Vault, 1828: Door.*

23. *Peter Roberts Vault, 1828. Interior with five coffins.*

24. Overcrowded Room, 1847.

25. The Ten Roman Catholic Clergymen who died of Typhus Fever
in 1847.

26. *Canon Edward Kenrick, 1851–1860: Memorial Plaque.*

27. *Sixth Station of the Cross: Kenrick Memorial.*

28. Fr P. J. Phelan, 1860–1864.

29. Fr J. Hawksworth, 1864–1868.

30. Canon Edward Goethals, 1868–1921: 1899 Portrait.

31. *Monsignor James Nugent with the Fifth Irish Volunteers outside St Patrick's before embarkation for the Second Boer War, 1899.*

32. *Fr William Weston, curate, 1914–1922.*

33. *Fr Michael Timmons, 1921–1928.*

34. *Canon Arthur Madden, 1928–1942.*

35. Monsignor Laurence Curry, 1942–1975.

36. Fr Thomas Lynch, 1975–1977.

37. Fr Joseph Marsh, 1977–1981.

38. Canon Leo Stoker, 1981–1998.

39. *Rialto Cinema, destroyed in Toxteth Riots, 1981.*

40. *Fr Patsy Foley, 1998–2002.*

41. Fr Kenny Hyde, 2002–2008.

42. Fr John Southworth, 2008–2018.

43. *Fr Silviu Climent, 2018.*

44. *Boys from St Patrick's School, c 1900.*

45. St Patrick's Choir, 1923.

46. St Patrick's Boys' School, 1923.

47. St Patrick's Infants' School, Group I, 1923.

47. St Patrick's Infants' Schools, Group II, 1923.

48. St Patrick's Teachers, 1923.

49. *Teachers and Pupils of St Patrick's Infants' School, Park Place, 1978.*

50. *St Patrick's Primary Department, South Chester Street, 1978.*

51. *St Patrick's Primary School, 2020.*

52. *Aerial View of St Patrick's Church and Primary School, after 1980.*

53. Brancker's statue of St Patrick on West front,
awaiting restoration, 2020.

54. West front ensemble: Memorial Cross, Dedication Plaque and
Statue.

55. *Archbishop Patrick O'Regan of Adelaide.*

56. *Adolf and William Patrick Hitler.*

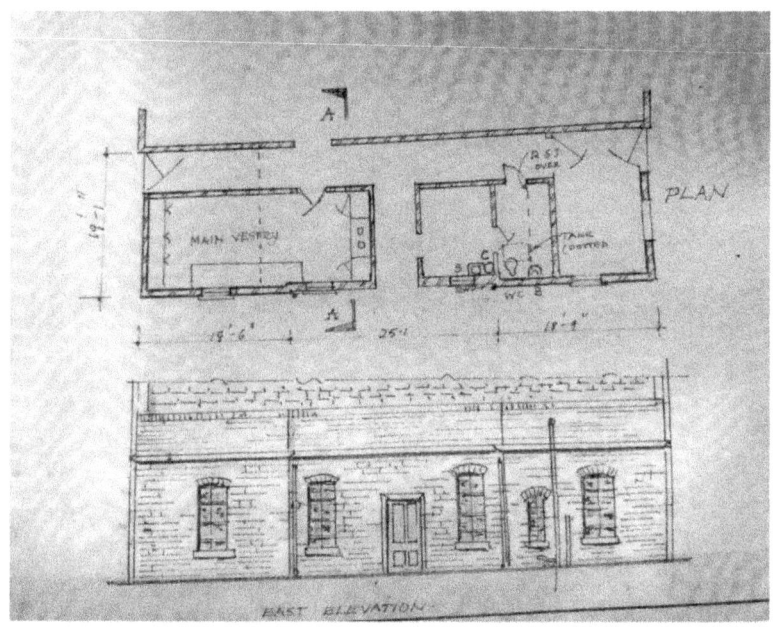

57. *Original Sacristy, March 1969.*

58. Recast bell.

59. Statue painted 2020.

60. *Statue cleaned 2021.*

61. *Bell tower before works 2020.*

62. *Bell tower under restoration 2021.*

63. *Bell tower restored 2021.*

64. *Church and school 2021.*

65. *Restored statue with missing finger 2021.*

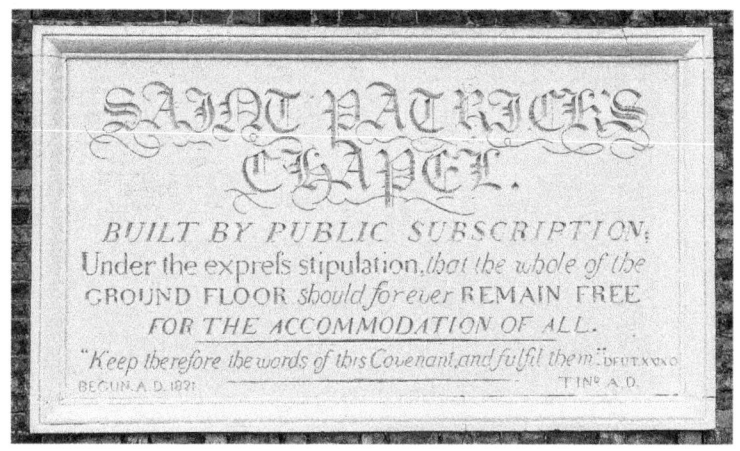

66. *Restored plaque 2021.*

Lightning Source UK Ltd.
Milton Keynes UK
UKHW011056180822
407485UK00003B/83